Red Lion Square, 18 May 2022, the 150th anniversary of Bertrand Russell's birth. We gathered at nearby Conway Hall to mark the occasion and inaugurate the Bloomsbury Chapter of the Bertrand Russell Society. Photo: Alva White

AF083415

The Spokesman

Our Common Security

Edited by Tony Simpson and Tom Unterrainer

Published by Spokesman for the
Bertrand Russell Peace Foundation
Ken Coates: Editor 1970 to 2010

Spokesman 151   **2022**

CONTENTS

Editorial	3	
China and Ukraine	5	*John Gittings*
Ukraine Wars	10	*Richard Falk*
A Ukraine Wars People's Tribunal?	16	*Richard Falk*
For Washington, war never ends	23	*Diana Johnstone*
Europe and NATO Expansion	31	*Frank Blackaby*
Definition	41	*Raymond Williams*
Remember your humanity	47	*Pamela Wood*
Common Security 2022	55	
Nuclear-weapon-free zones	78	*Palme Commission*
NWFZ: How they work	82	*Tom Unterrainer*
A Soviet View	87	*A. N. Kalyadin*
The F Word	94	*Mhairi Black MP*
Reviews	96	*Ross Bradshaw, Barry Baldwin, Becky Alexis-Martin, Stephen Winfield, Helen Jackson, Gregory Woods*
The Rosary	114	*Colm Tóibín*
END Info	115	*Ludo De Brabander, Joseph Gerson, Hans Kristensen*

Cover: A mother and baby girl were amongst those killed in Russia's missile attack on the port city of Odessa on 24 April 2022. This anonymous and spontaneous homage to the innocent dead soon appeared in protest in Moscow.

ISSN 1367 7748   ISBN 978 0 85124 9094

Subscriptions
Institutions £40.00 (ex UK)
£33.00 (UK)
Individuals £20.00 (UK)
£25.00 (ex UK)

A CIP catalogue record for this book is available from the British Library

Published by
The Bertrand Russell Peace Foundation Ltd,
5 Churchill Park,
Nottingham, NG4 2HF
England
Tel. 0115 9708318
email:
editor@russfound.org
www.spokesmanbooks.org
www.russfound.org

Editorial Board
John Daniels
Kate Fleet
Stuart Holland
Henry McCubbin
Abi Rhodes
Regan Scott

FSC
Mixed Sources
Product group from well-managed forests and other controlled sources

Cert no. SGS-COC-006541
www.fsc.org
© 1996 Forest Stewardship Council

Editorial

Our Common Security

President Putin's nuclear threats become more explicit: 'If someone decides to intervene in the ongoing events from the outside and create unacceptable strategic threats for us, they should know that our response to those oncoming blows will be swift, lightning fast,' he said in publicly broadcast remarks in St Petersburg in April 2022. 'We have the tools for this—ones that no one can brag about. And we won't brag. We will use them if needed. And I want everyone to know this. We have already taken all the decisions on this.' His political audience applauded.

Russia's criminal war on Ukraine has rapidly taken on the character of potential nuclear confrontation. In late February, shortly after Russia's extended invasion of Ukraine from the north, east and south, Putin publicly put Russia's 'deterrence' forces on special alert. He didn't use the word 'nuclear', but those are the weapons he's told them to prepare. In breaking the nuclear taboo, Putin exposes the duplicity of nuclear 'deterrence', which really means threatening mass death. In 1945, the United States twice visited mass death on Japan, and has refined its nuclear weapons practice ever since. When, in response to his recent threats, the French Foreign Minister reminded Putin that NATO is a nuclear-armed alliance, the threat of mass death was implicit in his few words.

Nor does the pretence that NATO is purely defensive and no threat to Russia help us to perceive clearly the acute danger we are in. Long ago, Putin absorbed the lessons of NATO's attack on Yugoslavia in 1999 and he is hyper sensitive to any perceived aggression, even while he orders Russia's military to mount its deadly and illegal assault on Ukraine. He publicly told President Macron that 'there would be no winners'. He publicly threatened anyone who interfered in Russia's war on Ukraine that they would suffer unprecedented consequences. Now he orders Russia's high command to actively participate in nuclear blackmail. NATO's Secretary-General decries such nuclear 'rhetoric', but who can be certain that Putin is bluffing? The fearful possibility is that Putin may be approaching the point where he decides he has nothing to lose by breaking the taboo and using some of Russia's many nuclear weapons. 'Deterrence' will have flipped.

Meanwhile, Putin's nuclear threats elicit some changes in US military operations. Scheduled testing of an intercontinental ballistic missile is postponed in case it disturbs the delicate balance of mutual threats of mass death. Such caution is prudent when taboos on nuclear threats and possible use are broken. But, in one telling sign of long-term escalation, storage bunkers for nuclear weapons are to be upgraded at the US airbase at Lakenheath, some 25 miles from Cambridge in Eastern England, where the United States has recently deployed its state-of-the-art F35 *Lightning* aircraft.

As a nuclear-armed alliance, NATO is somewhat constrained in militarily assisting Ukraine in its hour of need. Stalled columns of Russian fighting vehicles presented easy targets from the air, but NATO did not dispatch its substantial air power against them for fear of engaging Russia directly and triggering Putin's nuclear arsenal, which includes many so-called 'tactical' warheads — 'deterrence' flips to 'escalate to de-escalate', as the expression goes in Russian nuclear military doctrine. Where does that end?

Echoing Presidents Gorbachev and Reagan speaking in 1985, the leaders of China, France, Russia, UK and USA jointly and publicly affirmed, in January 2022, that a nuclear war cannot be won and must never be fought. They reaffirmed the importance of addressing nuclear threats. What changed in a few weeks? How is it that such threats are repeated and nuclear weapons made ready for use?

We remind the five leaders of their recent pledge. Our common security is at stake. They are surely right that a nuclear war cannot be won. Nor must it ever be fought. We call on them to honour their joint commitment to prevent nuclear war and avoid arms races. In recent years, Russia, the Unites States and the United Kingdom have steadily lowered the 'threshold' to be crossed when ordering the use of nuclear weapons. They openly state that nuclear devices could be used in response to threatened non-nuclear attacks such as 'conventional', biological, chemical or cyber. Nuclear capabilities are closely integrated with 'conventional' force in current military doctrine. 'Useable' nuclear weapons, hypersonic missiles, artificial intelligence, armed drones and cyberwarfare are all part of the contemporary battlespace – including a nuclear one.

For the sake of humanity, Russia should cease its aggression and withdraw from Ukraine without delay. Millions of people in Russia, Ukraine and the wider world know that war is not the answer to Eurasia's common and enduring need for security. The work to build peace and security begins again. In doing so, it is timely to recall that, long ago, Bertrand Russell confronted humankind's peril from nuclear weapons and appealed 'as a human being to human beings: remember your humanity, and forget the rest'.

Tony Simpson

China and Ukraine

An ambiguous diplomacy

John Gittings

For many years, John Gittings was a distinguished journalist on The Guardian *newspaper. He is now a foremost peace historian. His landmark book,* The Glorious Art of Peace, *should be in every peace activist's library (Oxford, £12.99).*

Three weeks before President Putin invaded Ukraine, he arrived in Beijing to attend the winter Olympics and promptly issued a joint statement with Xi Jinping that glowed with friendship. Both sides agreed to set up a "new kind of relationship" that was "superior" to their Cold War alliance, and in which there were "no 'forbidden' areas of cooperation". As usual, the Chinese government and media offered no elaboration on the meaning of this: outside China it was widely interpreted to mean that Putin had promised to take no action on Ukraine till the winter Olympics were over, and that Xi had agreed not to object to whatever action he might take.

Under Xi Jinping, Chinese policy statements are even more rigid and formulaic than before, and the old skills of Beijingology have come back into tiresome play. So when, two weeks (7 March) after the Russian invasion, Foreign Minister Wang Yi said he wished to stress "the China-Russia relationship is… based on non-alliance, non-confrontation and non-targeting of any third party", the words were clearly significant – but in what way? Was this simply an elaboration of the "new kind of relationship", or was it an effort to distance China from an invasion that even at this early date was not going well? If so, was this distancing genuine or just designed to create the illusion of neutrality?

Several months further on, it remains hard to decide exactly where China stands on the biggest challenge for sixty years to the future peace of the world. Our judgement is complicated by uncertainty as to the power balance in Beijing. Did Xi promise too much to Putin and is now on the defensive against internal critics, or does he remain firmly in control but hampered by his commitment and uncertain how to act?

My own view – and no one has the facts to offer much more – is that it was in the interests of both Putin and Xi to avoid specifics in discussing Ukraine. While Putin would not want to alarm China in advance of his intended action, Xi would not want to be compromised by learning too much. Xi may have calculated initially that a successful and swift Russian invasion would put the US and its allies on the defensive, clearing the path for the Chinese invasion of Taiwan. If so, that calculation has now been proved faulty.

China's world view

It would be wrong to see China's position only through one aspect of a much larger picture for Beijing. Central to this is China's mistrust of US policies in its own region, so that NATO's expansion into the former Soviet bloc is viewed very much through an East Asian lens. China's rise to great power status was encouraged by the US in the 1990s; entry into the WTO (achieved in 2001) was seen by both as paving the way for cooperation rather than conflict, The two countries, said President Jiang Zemin in 1997, shared "broad common interests and shoulder common responsibility on many important questions", a view reciprocated by President Clinton when he visited Beijing. The US mood began to change with the arrival of George W Bush: China was viewed increasingly as a global rival while Chinese negative views of the US, still recalling American support for Chiang Kai-shek, began to resurface. The decline of trust on both sides since then is a complex story, but at heart is American fear of a strong China – which it had helped to build up – and Chinese mistrust, which can be taken to extremes, of what is perceived as America's ambition to deny it its rightful place in the world.

Chinese strategists have long been accustomed to judge specific challenges on the basis of a broad view of the dominant world contradictions – an approach that goes back to Mao Zedong's strategies even before the 1949 victory. In its crudest form it amounts to this: who is China's enemy, who is China's friend, and how can those countries lying in between, in the "intermediate" zone, be won over? From this perspective the US is the foe and Russia, for all its failings, the friend, while Europe is one of the principal "intermediate" zones. The picture is not so clear as in the past: some Chinese analysts see the EU as a third power centre while Eastern and Southern Europe are a "middle zone" in contention. Negative views of the US are only reinforced by the reciprocal hostility of Washington towards China. Thus although the US might be expected to seek better relations with Beijing today to offset Russian influence, instead Secretary of State Anthony Blinken declares that in spite of the invasion of Ukraine, "China remains the greatest challenger of the US and its allies" (*New York Times,* 26 May 2022). Such statements allow China to claim the high ground, asserting in response that "it is never China's goal to surpass or replace the US". This moderate diplomatic tone is not reflected in the Chinese media, nor indeed in social media postings from the Chinese Ministry of Foreign Affairs, that routinely denounce, mock and vilify the US.

China's Ukraine policy
Chinese policy has been spelt out along the following lines:

1. China supports the principle of territorial integrity and sovereignty (understood to include Ukraine). It also firmly supports the UN Charter. However, China believes that security of one nation must not be achieved at the expense of the security of all (a coded reference to NATO expansion).
2. China is "deeply worried and saddened" by the war (Premier Li Keqiang, 11 March) and wishes to see peace restored as soon as possible. This should be achieved through negotiation, and China is working to bring this about – but it is doing so "in its own way" (the same phrase is used invariably but without elaboration).
3. China deplores the humanitarian disaster now occurring in Ukraine, and is providing assistance.

In practical terms at the time of writing (late May 2022), China has done little to translate these principles into practice:

At the UN: China abstained in the two key votes of February 28th and March 2nd, in the Security Council (SC) and General Assembly (GA) respectively, that condemned Russia's invasion. The SC resolution was modified (using the word "invasion" rather than "aggression") to win Chinese support, but failed to do so. The GA resolution, approved by 141 votes (73 percent of the UN membership), spoke of "aggression", citing numerous provisions of the Charter and international law. China objected that the UN should take account of the "complex historical background" to Ukraine, and should safeguard "the universal security of all parties". These issues would have been addressed in a South African resolution that failed to win enough preliminary votes to be discussed, and for which China would presumably have voted.

In April China failed to offer support to the Secretary-General's mission to Moscow and Ki´iv – nor did Britain or any other major power – and the failure of this mission led Antonio Guterres to conclude that there was currently no prospect of a diplomatic solution.

Negotiations: China has called on occasion for an "immediate ceasefire", notably in a joint foreign ministers' statement (25 March) with India. There is no hint that this has been raised directly with Russia, or indeed what substance there is to any dialogue with Putin. Some early discussions with Western leaders seem to have touched upon possible security guarantees for a neutral Ukraine, but this too has faded. China's core position was set out in a dialogue between President Xi and EU leaders (1st April) in general terms. The root cause of the Ukraine crisis, said Xi, was "the regional security tensions in Europe that have built up over the years", and a solution must be found "to accommodate the legitimate security concerns of all relevant parties." The crisis should be handled properly, and one should not "take the wrong medicine, or focus on just one aspect of the issue…. The more critical the situation, the greater the need to stay level-headed." The need for an immediate ceasefire, or for any other concrete action, was not mentioned in any reports of this meeting.

President Zelensky, in a video link with the Davos Conference (25 May), said that "at the moment" Ukraine was satisfied with China's policy which was "better than helping the Russian Federation". He admitted that "China has not taken any steps against Ukraine" but equally that no steps against Ukraine had been observed. We do not know whether Zelensky has received any private assurances from Beijing, but his careful choice of words underlines the ambiguity of Chinese policy.

Humanitarian aid: China has made much of its commitment to provide such aid, but by the end of May, Beijing had only reported the shipment of two tranches of aid, both in March, totalling US$2.5 million in value. (Chinese television reported a third tranche of which there is no other record). While Ukraine will be grateful for what it can get, this has the appearance of a token commitment rather than outright support.

Dissenting voices

Chinese dissent from the official line of what may be termed "pro-Russian neutrality" has been scarce, and has struggled against strict guidelines to the official media and censorship of social media. An early flurry of criticism on *WeChat* and other social media was quickly stifled. Official newspapers and television have been forbidden to use the term "invasion" or even "war." — minor exceptions to the rule seem to be accidental.

China's apparent neutral stance is undermined by the constant recycling of Russian propaganda, as notably over the Bucha massacre. China said it was suspending judgement until an impartial enquiry has been conducted, but its media repeated Russian claims that the civilian victims were actors, or had been shot by Ukrainian forces, while failing to publish any contrary narrative from Ukrainian sources..

By the end of May, only a handful of critics of Russian aggression and China's stance could be identified. A call on Russia to stop the war issued early on by five academics was quickly censored. Two other academics have expressed concern in a more acceptable form. Wang Huiwao, president of the Center for China Globalization, contributed a guest essay to the *New York Times* (13 March) under the headline "It's Time to Offer Russia an Offramp: China Can Help with That". Hu Wei, an advisor at the State Council Counsellor's Office, published a commentary in the US-*China Perception Monitor* (12 March) concluding that "China is the only country in the world with this capability [to stop Putin's adventure], and it must give full play to this unique advantage." Over the next two months, there were no more expressions of even such moderate dissent.

Hu was right that China is the only country that can rein in Putin, and academic and business professionals in the US and Europe with connections to China have been urging this upon their Chinese contacts and friends. Some of the responses reflect considerable disquiet, but an understandable reluctance to speak out.

In conclusion

The call for China to seek an immediate ceasefire and international mediation over Ukraine needs to be matched by a similar call on Western governments, particularly the US and Britain, not to insist on pursuing the war till a (probably unachievable) Ukrainian victory. This readiness to fight to the last Ukrainian is immoral and dangerous, and both countries, together with China, have a special duty under the UN Charter as Security Council members to work for international peace. This should mean supporting the Secretary-General in his mediating role, mobilising opinion in the General Assembly for an immediate ceasefire, and beginning to discuss a possible UN peace-keeping force. The UN is only "useless", as self-declared realists proclaim, if it is not used. To stop this terrible war that poses an existential risk to the world will require a profound change in thinking and far more active diplomacy, both in Beijing and in Western capitals: it is undoubtedly an uphill task, but it has to be undertaken.

Ukraine Wars

A geopolitical perspective

Richard Falk

This article is a somewhat modified version of a talk given on March 9th, 2022 at a session of the Global Studies Colloquium, University of California, Santa Barbara, convened by Professor Jan Nederveen Pieterse. I regret not having a transcript as a series of challenging questions followed my remarks, including several participants in Europe. Covid has made transnational dialogue much more of a common and enriching feature of intellectual activity on university campuses.

RF, 12/03/2022

When we agreed on a theme for my presentation, we were in a pre-Ukraine world. In the interim, developments in Ukraine, including the imprudent US-led provocations, Russian aggression against a sovereign state has created a severe humanitarian crisis in a country of over 44 million people. The confrontational Western response, by way of sanctions, and a surging Russophobia, has produced a win/lose calculus rather than striving for partial win/win political outcomes. I would identify such outcomes as restoring respect for Ukrainian sovereign rights (ceasefire, orderly Russian withdrawal; reconstruction assistance; emergency humanitarian aid) coupled with a commitment by Ukraine to never join NATO or allow Western troops or weaponry to be deployed on its soil. In addition, a commitment to allow self-government in Eastern Ukraine and the protection of human rights in Donbas region in accord with the reinvigoration of the Minsk Agreements of 2014-15 are required. The West's refusal to practise

Richard Falk is professor emeritus of international law at Princeton University and was Professor of Global Law, Queen Mary University of London. He served a six-year term as United Nations Special Rapporteur on the situation of human rights in Palestinian territories.

win/win diplomacy is suggestive of an absence of political and moral imagination at a time in world history when the resources and energies of the world need to be dedicated to global problem-solving as never before, and not be diverted by geopolitical dramas of the kind that has been tragically unfolding in Ukraine since February 24th.

Geopolitics is often invoked vaguely and abstractly, frequently given diverse meaning, and thus needs to be explained. Geopolitics is most usefully understood as referencing the behaviour of dominant states: what used to be called Great Powers. There is a confusion embedded in the discipline of International Relations, which generally refers to a state-centric world order based on juridical equality as exemplified by international law, and has been recently mystified in the political discourse of the US Secretary of State, Antony Blinken. This high official insists that US foreign policy adheres to the restraints of a rule-governed international order, while that of its rivals, China and Russia, does not, and that for him makes all the difference. In actuality, the reality of geopolitics is most manifest in war/peace or international security contexts where all Great Powers throughout the world history of several centuries privilege their strategic priorities over adherence to rules or norms of general application.

At the end of World War II there were basically two geopolitical actors – the US & USSR. Additionally, through the strength of Winston Churchill's personality and the vitality of the trans-Atlantic alliance, the UK was treated as a third geopolitical actor. France was later added as a courtesy urged by Churchill to avoid Britain enduring the loneliness of being the predominant colonial power. China as the most populous country and the sole representative of the Global South was the final state admitted to this exclusive club of geopolitical actors, who not only became the five permanent members of the United Nations Security Council, but were also the first five countries to develop and possess nuclear weapons. Franklin Roosevelt exerted American influence, backed by Stalin, to ensure that the United Nations would be established in a manner that took account of the institutional failures of the League of Nations that had been brought into existence after World War I to keep the peace. FDR attributed the failure of the League as arising from its Westphalian state-centric framing of authority.

Instead of juridical equality as the dominant organizing principle, Roosevelt favoured the establishment of a hybrid institution: geopolitical primacy for the Security Council (SC) endowed with sole authority to reach and implement, if necessary by force, binding decisions. Westphalian statism was relied upon to legitimate claims of authority in the General Assembly and rest of UN System, yet limited in its efforts to influence behaviour to advisory and recommendatory authority that has turned out to have had inconsequential impacts in relation to the most pressing items on the global policy agenda.

Additional support for hybridity came from the Soviet Union that sought not only Permanent Membership in the Security Council but structural assurances that it would not be victimized by a tyranny of the majority composed of anti-Communist Western-leaning countries. Soviet concerns were set forth as part of the justification for granting a right of veto to the permanent five (P5). The central idea was to frame the peace and security priorities of the new UN in a manner that provided clearer ample political space for the practice of geopolitics within the four walls of the Organization. It is not surprising that this accommodation of geopolitics produced an impasse at the UN, approaching political paralysis during the Cold War. It also perversely meant that the P5 were constitutionally empowered to opt out of compliance with international law whenever their strategic interests so decreed by simply casting a veto blocking a Security Council decision.

It should be noted that a quite differerent approach was taken in the economic sphere of the Bretton Woods institutions of the World Bank and International Monetary Fund, where Western primacy for market economies was achieved by weighted voting and leadership traditions proportionally based on capital contributions. Such a capitalist consensus did indeed lead to a rule-based international liberal order, which contrasted with the contested ideological combat zone of post-1945 geopolitics.

Roosevelt's vision of the UN was vindicated to some extent by achieving and maintaining universality of membership throughout the entirety of the Cold War. Providing a comfort zone for geopolitics did overcome one of the principal procedural weaknesses of the state-centric League. The League suffered from non-participation (US), withdrawal (USSR), and expulsion (Germany), arguably the most important international actors between the two world wars.

The most hopeful part of FDR's vision for the UN proved irrelevant and naïve. Roosevelt was hopeful that countries with diverse ideologies that had cooperated so effectively in responding to the fascist challenge in the war would extend their alliance to peacetime. He believed, or maybe just hoped, that the victors in World War II would take on the less onerous challenges of peacetime. In retrospect, it seems clear that those who led the peace diplomacy after World War II underestimated the intensity of antagonistic geopolitical ambitions that had been temporarily subdued to address the common threat posed by fascism, and that the removal of that threat made possible the resumption of fierce geopolitical rivalry between the two military superpowers.

The Cold War, despite its periodic crises, proxy wars, and arms races managed to avoid a 'Third World War' by producing a relatively stable geopolitical balance of power based on two principal elements: deterrence (mutual assured destruction) and respect for each other's spheres of influence. The risks of war during this period arose over different perceptions of respective degrees of control over spheres of influence, as in the Cuban Missile Crisis of 1962 and the interplay of nationalisms and ideological affinities in the three divided countries of Korea and Vietnam – that led to horribly destructive proxy wars – and Germany that produced recurrent crises that endangered peace in scary ways. War prevention was more successful in Europe where respective spheres of influence accepted hostile interventions by the Soviet Union in Eastern Europe and more subtly by the US in Western Europe.

What might be called 'the geopolitics of peace' during the Cold War reflected patterns of assertion and restraint that reflected the prevailing geopolitical structure: the presence of nuclear weapons, and the collapse of European colonialism. The structural reality of the Cold War period was captured by a militarist understanding of geopolitics in the nuclear age, and by the imaginary 'bipolarity.' Such abstractions, unless elaborated, obscure the role of geopolitical leadership, internal cohesion and governance, and perceptions of the adversary. Yet 'bipolarity' gives a more instructive view of geopolitics than does an emphasis on the Permanent 5 in the UN setting, and has prevailed in the academic International Relations literature.

The collapse of the Soviet Union led to what the right-wing neoconservatives in the US heralded as the onset of 'a unipolar moment,' which meant that the logic of balance and deterrence no longer applied, especially in conflicts within the spheres of influence bordering on China and Russia. Balance was replaced by the logic of dominance and asymmetry. A triumphalist atmosphere emerged in the US during the 1990s conveyed by such phrases as 'the end of history,' 'the second [New] American Century,' 'the doctrine of enlargement,' and 'democracy promotion.' No longer was geopolitics conceived largely in regional terms, but rather as a global undertaking of a single political actor, the United States, the first truly 'global state' whose security zone encompassed the planet.

But there were problems with operationalizing a Monroe Doctrine for the world: the potency of nationalist resistance neutralizing over time the impact of military superiority enjoyed by the intervening geopolitical actor, a revision of the balance of forces as between intervenors and national sites of struggle recently evident in Iraq and Afghanistan; the fact that China's challenge was not primarily military, and thus could not be 'deterred' by force alone; the growing Russian resentment at being hemmed in and threatened by the geopolitical acrobatics of unipolarity.

One further observation of a conceptual nature: world order is constituted by two normative logics: a geopolitical logic based on inequality of states and a juridical logic based on their equality. For relations based on equality, international law provides a framework; for those based on inequality, strategic priorities – including war avoidance – underpin action. Bipolarity proved to be relatively resilient, unipolarity turned out to be dysfunctional, producing massive human suffering, widespread devastation and human displacement while frustrating the pursuit and attainment of geopolitical goals.

Before the Ukraine crisis, there seemed to be forming a new geopolitical configuration based on somewhat different patterns of alignment: 'containment' was being resurrected in relation to China and focusing on the defense of South Asia, including the islands, with a less Euro-centric alliance on both sides. Instead of NATO v Warsaw Pact there is the relations of US, India, UK, and Australia. Russia seemed to be replacing East Europe as the principal ally or partner of China suggesting a new phase of bipolarity and the onset of a second cold war.

Putin's attack on Ukraine drastically challenged that playbill, or so it now seems. He had previously pledged 'the end of the unipolar world,' and seemed to mean this primarily in relation to the Russian sphere of influence along its Western borders, starting with Ukraine. Such a geopolitical approach is running into some comparable obstacles to those encountered by the US with respect to unipolarity. China is placed in an awkward position of conflicting priorities, balancing US encroachments and hegemonic geopolitics, yet uphold the sanctity of territorial sovereignty, the major premise of Westphalian world order.

One can conjecture that if a diplomatic solution is soon found for Ukraine, the Sino-Russian defensive geopolitics will revive. The Trump factor cannot be discounted in the near future, and with it a return to a geopolitical realignment scheme that was friendlier to Russia and more economistic in character, viewing China as the more troublesome rival of the US from the perspective of trade, investment, and technological innovation.

What seems clear is that the 30-year aftermath of the Cold War is ending amid the ruins and humanitarian crisis unfolding in Ukraine. What comes next depends on many factors, including the impingement of unmet global challenges not previously prominent on geopolitical agendas, yet posing dire threats to the future stability of planetary political, economic, and ecological arrangements if they are not treated as matters of urgency.

First published at https://richardfalk.org/2022/03/12/the-ukraine-war-a-geopolitical-perspective/

Ukraine: Stop the Carnage, Build the Peace!

In March 2022, Just World Educational held a series of eight webinars on the international crisis sparked by Russia's February invasion of Ukraine. The sessions were co-hosted by JWE  President Helena Cobban and Board Member Richard Falk; in each one, they conducted a broad public conversation on issues raised by the crisis with superbly well-qualified and thoughtful guests.

The multimedia records of all these conversations can be viewed at bit.ly/JWE-UkraineCrisis. Policy Recommendations arising from these conversations are as follows:

1. Ukraine-wide ceasefire now!

2. An embargo on arms shipments into Ukraine by all countries.

3. Start negotiations now, involving all relevant parties, for a lasting peace arrangement for Ukraine, and commit to completion within six months.

4. Monitoring and verification of the ceasefire and arms embargo to be led by the United Nations and the OSCE, or any other party acceptable to both Ukraine and Russia.

5. Immediate aid for rebuilding in Ukraine, including for agriculture, ports, residential areas, and related systems.

6. Immediate international talks on implementation of 1970 Nuclear Non-Proliferation Treaty, under which all signatory states including the United States and Russia committed to complete nuclear disarmament, and a call for all governments to support the 2017 Treaty on the Prohibition of Nuclear Weapons .

7. Leaders of NATO countries should oppose all manifestations of Russophobia.

8. The United States should give up all efforts at regime change in Russia.

A full report on the conversations can be accessed at justworldeducational.org

A Ukraine Wars People's Tribunal?

Richard Falk

A somewhat modified version was published online in CounterPunch on May 6, 2022 under the title 'Toward a Ukraine Wars People's Tribunal'. The most important change is the insistence that the Geopolitical War taking place under the rubric of the Ukraine War is different and far more dangerous than what is being described as a 'proxy war.' Also important is the growing evidence that the inflammatory nature of Biden's tactics in the Geopolitical War, especially the endorsement of 'a victory scenario' compounds the dangers, including heightening the risk that nuclear weapons will be used. What is needed is for civil society to frame with a sense of urgency 'a peace scenario' with as many specifications of its character as possible. I consider the proposal to form a civil society tribunal a step in this direction.

RF

Towards a People's Ukraine Wars Tribunal

The deepening current Ukraine Crisis is properly linked to the Russian aggression that commenced with a massive military attack against Ukraine on February 24, 2022, although it should not cover up the provocative developments of preceding years that prepared the way for what has erupted. The Russian attack has continued to ravage the country since, including inducing a refugee flow numbering several million. There is a broad consensus around the world that such aggression is a criminal violation of international law, and while noting the irresponsible nature of NATO provocations, it is widely agreed, fail to

WORLD TRIBUNAL ON IRAQ

MAKING THE CASE AGAINST WAR

edited by Müge Gürsöy Sökmen
introductions by Arundhati Roy and Richard Falk

provide Russia with a legally, morally, or even politically persuasive rationale with respect to accountability for such a violent encroachment on Ukrainian sovereign rights and territorial integrity. At the same time, from the outset of these events there was much more limited international support for the American led punitive response by NATO featuring harsh comprehensive sanctions amounting to 'economic warfare,' shipment of weaponry to the beleaguered country, dehumanization of Putin and Russo-phobic propaganda, along with silence about recourse to a diplomacy directed at stopping the killing and devastation. In the background of the two-level war was the related internal struggle within Ukraine between dominant indigenous forces in the Western part of the country and the Russian-speaking Ukrainians who are the majority in the industrial heartland of the country in the Dombas East.

As Russian military operations proceeded, perceptions of the core conflict began to change. What seemed at first a simple war of aggression, to be followed by belligerent operation, became by successive phases a geopolitical war between the United States and Russia, with strategic goals quite apart from the outcome of events in Ukraine, as well as heightening costs of the encounter for the entire world, including the people of Ukraine and especially the extreme poor everywhere. And while Washington bears the main responsibility for this shift, the Russian response was also irresponsible– not compromising war goals and recourse to veiled threats of nuclear warfare emanating from Moscow and Putin. Yet the essential character in this elevation of the war strategy to a geopolitical level of engagement is the rather explicit American shift in its policy entailing less of an emphasis upon bolstering Ukrainian resistance to Russian aggression and far more about inflicting a stunning geopolitical defeat on Russia and at the same time revitalizing post-Cold War transatlantic unity through a reaffirmation of the benefits of the NATO alliance in a global context where Russia is once more cast as the enemy of Western democracy.

It is important to understand that this Geopolitical War raises the stakes in Ukraine much higher than the prevailing tendency to view the second level war between the US and Russia as a 'proxy war.' A proxy war conceives of the strategic stakes in terms of the outcome of the conflict on the ground, whose overt antagonists are Russia and Ukraine. Conceiving of this confrontation as a geopolitical war calls attention to the much larger strategic consequences and risks because what is at stake is the structure of power on a global scale, specifically this Geopolitical War will influence the struggle between the US, Russia, and China as to whether the global security will reflect unipolarity or multipolarity. It is easier for a country to accept defeat in a proxy war than in a geopolitical war, and herein lies embedded grave dangers of escalation.

Given such developments, the time has come for civil society initiatives to counter the disastrous global confrontation that is now endangering the world, and indeed even species survival prospects, in the pursuit of these geopolitical goals by the United States disguised somewhat by media complicity that continues to convey the impression that the Ukraine War is still only about the defence of Ukrainian sovereignty and territorial integrity, the daily war crimes attributable to the Russians, and the heroic and increasingly successful efforts of the Zelensky leadership and the courageous national unity of the Ukrainian people. I believe this is a basically deceptive and potentially dangerous image, including for Ukraine, and even for the main disseminator of hostile geopolitical propaganda, the US Government and consequently, the American people. Perhaps it comes as a disturbing surprise that only the political extremes of right and left are interpreting the Ukraine War as producing a global disaster that begun to spill across the borders of Ukraine, with far worse to come without even taking full account of the growing nuclear dangers. What has also become evident is the helplessness of peace-oriented approaches. Such voices are being shut out by mainstream media platforms, which is reinforced by the inability of the UN to act independently of a geopolitical consensus, and by inter-governmental impotence to safeguard human interest in face of the menacing moves by the most powerful states motivated by strong contradictory geopolitical goals.

In light of this line of interpretation, I am proposing the establishment of a civil society tribunal along the lines of the Russell Tribunal that brought independent critical voices to the fore during the Vietnam War, which had become the principal combat theatre of the Cold War in 1966-67. Although the tribunal was controversial at the time and of questionable relevance to ending that war, the Russell undertaking inspired many notable efforts along the same lines, most notably organized under the sponsorship of the Lelio Basso Foundation in Rome. Perhaps most notable was the elaborate series of such initiatives in response to US aggression against Iraq in 2003 culminating in the very significant Iraq War Tribunal of 2005. The proceedings of that event, appropriately held in Istanbul, can be beneficially studied to cast light on the policy dilemmas of the Ukraine Crisis. This self-funded event in Istanbul, orchestrated brilliantly by a group of Turkish progressive women citizens, brought together internationally prominent jurists and moral authority figures including

Arundhati Roy who served as the chair of the jury of conscience that sat in judgment, and rendered an opinion of lasting significance, especially for anti-war world tendencies.

It is my belief that such a tribunal devoted to passing judgment of the Ukraine Wars, constituted as a matter of urgency, is more important than any of these previous comparable civic events because the stakes for humanity are higher. The use of the plural for what is happening in Ukraine is not a typo, but reflects the view explained in my prior articles that the Ukraine Crisis can only be properly understood if interpreted as three interrelated wars with contradictory features: Level 1: Russia vs. Ukraine; Level: 2: US vs. Russia; Level 3: Western Ukraine vs. Dombas. It is for this reason that I am proposing here that the tribunal be named People's Tribunal on the Ukraine Wars, despite its awkwardness.

The case for such an initiative is not only to give expression to views of the Ukraine Crisis that take international law, geopolitical crime, and nuclear dangers seriously, but also in view of the political incapacity of the UN to act effectively and responsibly when geopolitical actors get heavily embroiled in such a violent conflict which threatens world peace generally and causes massive suffering throughout the world, especially in the least developed countries or in societies dependent on import of basic foodstuffs and energy for reliable supplies at affordable prices. Most of the people vulnerable to such a mega-crisis live in states that have hardly any influence in the formation of global policy, but often bear the heaviest weight of its shortcomings. At present a normative vacuum exists in response to the Ukraine Crisis. This leaves transnational civil society as the last, best hope to exert a responsibility to act, and indeed seize the opportunity to goad the formal political actors on the global stage to operationalize a peace scenario before it is too late.

Clarifying the Background

First, when it comes to war/peace issues there exist two operational sets of norms with respect to international relations: (1) International Law, binding on all sovereign states; (2) Geopolitics that privileges a few powerful states. The identity of geopolitical actors is not as clearly identified as is that of sovereign states, which is rather clearly signified by internationally recognized territorial boundaries and access to membership in the UN, now numbering 193, that is, virtually all. The most influential, yet still misleading, guideline as to geopolitical stature is contained in the UN Charter, taking the form of the right of veto conferred on the five Permanent Members of the Security Council (also known as the P-5) who happened to be the winners in World War II and also the five countries first to acquire nuclear weapons. As the composition of the P-5 has remained frozen in time for more than 77 years it is no longer descriptive of the geopolitical landscape, and never was. For this reason alone geopolitical identity is currently more blurred and problematic than earlier. Some P-5 members have declined in both hard and soft power since 1945, such as the UK and France, and seem to lack the capabilities and stature to qualify any longer as first tier geopolitical actors. In contrast, countries such as India, Japan, Germany, Brazil, Nigeria, Indonesia, South Africa have increased their capabilities and raised their stature in such ways as to seem existentially entitled to the status of 'geopolitical actors' at least regionally, and in some instances, globally.

From a normative point of view the distinction between international law and geopolitics is fundamental, and again is made clear by the significance of P-5 status within the UN framework which was designed to keep the peace after World War II. International law is applicable to every state, but is explicitly not obligatory for the P-5, which is what has made the UN so limited in its operational ability to provide humanity with a globally supervised war prevention system based on compliance with international law. Giving the Western states a veto was tantamount to acknowledging, as had been true for international relations in prior centuries, that the UN could not be expected to implement its own Charter norms if they collided with strategic interests of the P-5, but that compliance with these norms, if forthcoming at all would depend on geopolitical self-restraint or the counterforce of adversary geopolitical actors exerted outside the UN. A similar pattern of obstruction existed when Russia was the Soviet Union, yet its participation was seen as vital in 1945 if the UN was to enjoy global legitimacy premised on universal membership. Granting the USSR a right of veto was also a matter of protecting the country against its understandable anxiety about facing a Western majority on vital issues. As the decades have shown, the US in particular has used the veto (e.g. to shield Israel) or avoided the UN (as in the Vietnam War, NATO Kosovo War, and Iraq War of 2003) when it thought its proposed plan of action would be vetoed, or otherwise not supported. The UN was deliberately disempowered from any legal attempt to implement compliance with the UN Charter in relation to geopolitical actors, and the existential reality was not dissimilar from the pre-UN Westphalian structure of and experience with world order since the mid-17th century. Regulation of the use of force by the Great Powers, as they were formerly called, depended on a mixture of their self-restraint and what came to be known as 'the balance of power,' redesigned in the nuclear age as 'deterrence.' These nuclear dimensions are under challenge from many non-geopolitical states and world public opinion, most recently in the form of the 2021 Treaty on the Prohibition of Nuclear Weapons (TPNW). This initiative is so far limited in its impacts due to the distressing non-participation of any of the nine nuclear states, as well as their allies staking their security on the reliability of the 'the nuclear protectorate' provided by geopolitical actors.

A second set of related considerations can be identified as the 'Nuremberg Exception,' which can be interpreted as follows: a geopolitical actor loses its impunity with respect to international law if it is defeated in a major war. This attitude is evident in the course of the unfolding two-level war in Ukraine. The US at the highest level of its government has been condemning the Russian attack as a war crime that should engage criminal accountability of Putin, and others, if the International Criminal Court acts to fulfil its mandate. This can be viewed from one angle as a kind of 'winner takes all' feature of geopolitical order, or from another as gross hypocrisy by recourse to one-sided (in)justice beneath the banner of 'Victors' Justice.' Nuremberg would enjoy somewhat increased jurisprudential credibility if the US had demonstrated post-Nuremberg its own willingness to be held accountable under the frameworks of international criminal law or the codified version of the Nuremberg Principles, which do not acknowledge that a Nuremberg Exception exists, despite its persisting reality.

Thirdly, what is missing in this recital of the jurisprudential realities of international relations is the availability of a venue capable of a legitimate normative assessment of the behaviour of geopolitical actors whether they are on the winning or losing side in a major war. It is evident that the UN lacks the constitutional mandate and political independence to undertake such a challenge without a thorough overhaul in its authority structure. Such reforms would require the approval of the very actors whose behaviour would then become subject to international law, and these actors show no readiness to curtail their discretion. It is for this reason that the only way to close the accountability gap is to rely on civil society activism as a legitimate source of normative authority. One such responsive effort, used in the past, has been to convene a tribunal based on the authority of ordinary people as representatives of society to uphold international law in the event of the failure of the UN or governments to do so. In the setting of the Ukraine Crisis such a tribunal could be entrusted with investigating the three levels of the war from the perspective of international law, with the addition of an aspirational norm that extends the reach of the tribunal to the geopolitical domain.

At present, inter-governmentally generated international law not surprisingly fails to criminalize geopolitical wrongdoing. It is not surprising because throughout modern history geopolitical actors have been the principal architects of international law and vigilant about protecting their freedom of action along with their national interest more generally. I believe it has become desirable to posit the existence of a residual civil society legislative capacity somewhat analogous to the residual role of the General Assembly of the UN if an impasse is present in the Security Council with respect to a serious threat to international peace and security. On this basis a civil society endorsement of the concept of 'geopolitical crime' is justified to bring the US/Russia Geopolitical War within the ambit of the authority of The Ukraine Wars Tribunal.

There are two obvious weaknesses of this line of thinking that should be acknowledged. First, the Tribunal lacks any formal enforcement capability, although it could call for civil society boycotts and divestments that were effective in exerting transformative pressure on South Africa's apartheid regime. Secondly, the activist impulses that fund and make operational The Ukrainian Wars Tribunal are themselves self-consciously partisan or reflect the outlook of social movement, which is of course not qualitatively different than the deep biases of intergovernmental institutions. Such partisanship of this radical civic action will be subject to criticism from start to finish, which may yield a helpful debate about war, law, and accountability.

It is evident that this proposal is principally an undertaking whose effectiveness will in the first instance be registered symbolically rather than substantively in the sense that nothing immediate will change behaviourally in the prosecution and conduct of the three Ukrainian wars. Symbolic impacts should not be underestimated. The political outcomes in the most salient wars since 1945, including the epic struggles against colonialism, were politically controlled, often after many years of devastating warfare, by the weaker side if measured by material, especially military capabilities. I recall hearing the American president, Lyndon Johnson, in the mid-1960s boast that there was no way the United States could lose the war to Vietnam, 'a tenth-rate Asian power.' Symbolic venues shift power balances due to the commitments of people, and even alter the impacts of material interests over time. The struggles against slavery, racism, and patriarchy each manifest this dynamic. What at first seemed futile somehow became history!

In concluding, I hope some readers throughout the world will feel motivated enough to make the People's Ukraine Wars Tribunal a reality. It should be thought about as contributing to the imperative of framing A Peace Scenario that challenges the now ascendant Victory Scenario.

For Washington, war never ends

Diana Johnstone

Diana Johnstone was press secretary of the Green Group in the European Parliament from 1989 to 1996. In her book, Circle in the Darkness: Memoirs of a World Watcher *(Clarity Press, 2020), she recounts key episodes in the transformation of the German Green Party from a peace to a war party. Her other books include* Fools' Crusade: Yugoslavia, NATO and Western Delusions *(Pluto/Monthly Review) and in co-authorship with her father, Paul H. Johnstone,* From MAD to Madness: Inside Pentagon Nuclear War Planning *(Clarity Press).*

It goes on and on. The "war to end war" of 1914-1918 led to the war of 1939-1945, known as World War II. And that one has never ended either, mainly because for Washington it was the Good War, the war that made The American Century: why not the American Millennium?

The conflict in Ukraine may be the spark that sets off what we already call World War III. But this is not a new war. It is the same old war, an extension of the one we call World War II, which was not the same war for all those who took part. The Russian war and the American war were very, very different.

Russia's World War II

For Russians, the war was an experience of massive suffering, grief and destruction. The Nazi invasion of the Soviet Union was utterly ruthless, propelled by a racist ideology of contempt for the Slavs and hatred of "Jewish Bolsheviks." An estimated 27 million died, about two-thirds of them civilians. Despite overwhelming losses and suffering, the Red Army succeeded in turning the Nazi tide of conquest that had subdued most of Europe.

This gigantic struggle to drive the German invaders from their soil is known to Russians as the Great Patriotic War, nourishing a national pride that helped console the people for all they had been through. But whatever the pride in victory, the horrors of the war inspired a genuine desire for peace.

America's World War II

America's World War II (like World War I) happened somewhere else. That is a very big difference. The war enabled the United States to emerge as the richest and most powerful nation on earth. Americans were taught never to compromise, neither to prevent war ("Munich") nor to end one ("unconditional surrender" was the American way). Righteous intransigence was the fitting attitude of Good in its battle against Evil.

The war economy brought the US out of the depression. Military Keynesianism emerged as the key to prosperity. The Military-Industrial-Complex was born. To continue providing Pentagon contracts to every congressional constituency and guaranteed profits to Wall Street investors, it needed a new enemy. The Communist scare – the very same scare that had contributed to creating fascism – did the trick.

The Cold War: World War II Continued

In short, after 1945, for Russia, World War II was over. For the United States, it was not. What we call the Cold War was its voluntary continuation by leaders in Washington. It was perpetuated by the theory that Russia's defensive "Iron Curtain" constituted a military threat to the rest of Europe.

At the end of the war, the main security concern of Stalin was to prevent such an invasion from ever happening again. Contrary to Western interpretations, Moscow's ongoing control of Eastern European countries it had occupied on its way to victory in Berlin was not inspired so much by communist ideology as by determination to create a buffer zone as an obstacle to repeated invasion from the West.

Stalin respected the Yalta lines between East and West and declined to support the life and death struggle of Greek communists. Moscow cautioned leaders of large Western European Communist Parties to eschew revolution and play by the rules of bourgeois democracy. The Soviet occupation could be brutal but was resolutely defensive. Soviet sponsorship of peace movements was perfectly genuine.

The formation of the North Atlantic Treaty Organization (NATO) and the rearmament of Germany confirmed that, for the United States, the war in Europe was not entirely over. The lackadaisical US "de-Nazification" of its sector of occupied Germany was accompanied by an organized brain drain of Germans who could be useful to the United States in its rearmament and espionage (from Wernher von Braun to Reinhard Gehlen).

America's Ideological Victory

Throughout the Cold War, the United States devoted its science and industry to building a gigantic arsenal of deadly weapons, which wreaked devastation without bringing US victory in Korea or Vietnam. But military defeat did not cancel America's ideological victory.

The greatest triumph of American imperialism has been in spreading its self-justifying images and ideology, primarily in Europe. The dominance of the American entertainment industry has spread its particular blend of self-indulgence and moral dualism around the world, especially among youth. Hollywood convinced the West that World War II was won essentially by the US forces and their allies in the Normandy invasion.

America sold itself as the final force for Good as well as the only fun place to live. Russians were drab and sinister.

In the Soviet Union itself, many people were not immune to the attractions of American self-glorification. Some apparently even thought that the Cold War was all a big misunderstanding, and that if we are very nice and friendly, the West will be nice and friendly too. Mikhail Gorbachev was susceptible to this optimism.

Former US ambassador to Moscow Jack Matlock recounts that the desire to liberate Russia from the perceived burden of the Soviet Union was widespread within the Russian elite in the 1980s. It was the leadership rather than the masses who accomplished the self-destruction of the Soviet Union, leaving Russia as the successor state, with the nuclear weapons and UN veto of the USSR. under the alcohol-soaked presidency of Boris Yeltsin – and overwhelming US influence during the 1990s.

The New NATO

Russia's modernization over the past three centuries has been marked by controversy between "Westernizers" – those who see Russia's progress in emulation of the more advanced West – and "Slavophiles," who consider that the nation's material backwardness is compensated by some sort of spiritual superiority, perhaps based in the simple democracy of the traditional village.

In Russia, Marxism was a Westernizing concept. But official Marxism did not erase admiration for the "capitalist" West and in particular for America. Gorbachev dreamed of "our common European home" living some sort of social democracy. In the 1990s, Russia asked only to be part of the West.

What happened next proved that the whole "communist scare" justifying the Cold War was false. A pretext. A fake designed to perpetuate military Keynesianism and America's special war to maintain its own economic and ideological hegemony.

There was no longer any Soviet Union. There was no more Soviet communism. There was no Soviet bloc, no Warsaw Pact. NATO had no more reason to exist.

But in 1999, NATO celebrated its 50th anniversary by bombing Yugoslavia and thereby transforming itself from a defensive to an aggressive military alliance. Yugoslavia had been non-aligned, belonging neither to NATO nor the Warsaw Pact. It threatened no other country. Without authorization from the Security Council or justification for self-defence, the NATO aggression violated international law.

At the very same time, in violation of unwritten but fervent diplomatic promises to Russian leaders, NATO welcomed Poland, Hungary and the Czech Republic as new members. Five years later, in 2004, NATO took in Romania, Bulgaria, Slovakia, Slovenia and the three Baltic Republics. Meanwhile, NATO members were being dragged into war in Afghanistan, the first and only "defence of a NATO member" – namely, the United States.

Understanding Putin – Or Not

Meanwhile, Vladimir Putin had been chosen by Yeltsin as his successor, partly no doubt because as a former KGB officer in East Germany he had some knowledge and understanding of the West. Putin pulled Russia out of the shambles caused by Yeltsin's acceptance of American-designed economic shock treatment.

Putin put a stop to the most egregious rip-offs, incurring the wrath of dispossessed oligarchs who used their troubles with the law to convince the West that they were victims of persecution (example: the ridiculous Magnitsky Act).

On Feb. 11, 2007, the Russian Westernizer Putin went to a centre of Western power, the Munich Security Conference, and asked to be understood by the West. It is easy to understand, if one wants to. Putin challenged the "unipolar world" being imposed by the United States and emphasized Russia's desire to "interact with responsible and independent partners with whom we could work together in constructing a fair and democratic world order that would ensure security and prosperity not only for a select few, but for all."

The reaction of the leading Western partners was indignation, rejection, and a 15-year media campaign portraying Putin as some sort of demonic creature. Indeed, since that speech there have been no limits to Western media's insults directed at Putin and Russia. And in this scornful treatment we see the two versions of World War II. In 2014, world leaders gathered in Normandy to commemorate the 70th anniversary of the D-Day landings by US and British forces.

In fact, that 1944 invasion ran into difficulties, even though German forces were mainly concentrated on the Eastern front, where they were losing the war to the Red Army. Moscow launched a special operation precisely to draw German forces away from the Normandy front. Even so, Allied progress could not beat the Red Army to Berlin.

However, thanks to Hollywood, many in the West consider D-Day to be the decisive operation of World War II. To honour the event, Vladimir Putin was there and so was German Chancellor Angela Merkel. Then, in the following year, world leaders were invited to a lavish victory parade held in Moscow celebrating the 70th anniversary of the end of World War II. Leaders of the United States, Britain and Germany chose not to participate. This was consistent with an endless series of Western gestures of disdain for Russia and its decisive contribution to the defeat of Nazi Germany (it destroyed 80 per cent of the Wehrmacht.) On Sept. 19, 2019, the European Parliament adopted a resolution on "the importance of European remembrance for the future of Europe" which jointly accused the Soviet Union and Nazi Germany of unleashing World War II.

Vladimir Putin responded to this gratuitous affront in a long article on "The Lessons of World War II" published in English in *The National Interest* on the occasion of the 75th anniversary of the end of the war. Putin answered with a careful analysis of the causes of the war and its profound effect on the lives of the people trapped in the murderous 872-day Nazi siege of Leningrad (now Saint Petersburg), including his own parents whose two-year-old son was one of the 800,000 who perished.

Clearly, Putin was deeply offended by continual Western refusal to grasp the meaning of the war in Russia. "Desecrating and insulting the memory is mean," Putin wrote. "Meanness can be deliberate, hypocritical and pretty much intentional as in the situation when declarations commemorating the 75th anniversary of the end of the Second World War mention all participants in the anti-Hitler coalition except for the Soviet Union."

And all this time, NATO continued to expand eastward, more and more openly targeting Russia in its massive war exercises on its land and sea borders.

The US Seizure of Ukraine

The encirclement of Russia took a qualitative leap ahead with the 2014 seizure of Ukraine by the United States. Western media recounted this complex event as a popular uprising, but popular uprisings can be taken over by forces with their own aims, and this one was. The elected president, Viktor Yanukovych, was overthrown by violence a day after he had agreed to early elections in an accord with European leaders.

Billions of US dollars and murderous shootings by extreme right militants enforced a regime change openly directed by US Assistant Secretary of State

Victoria Nuland ("F___ the EU") producing a leadership in Kiev largely selected in Washington, and eager to join NATO (see *Spokesman* 124).

By the end of the year, the government of "democratic Ukraine" was largely in the hands of US-approved foreigners. The new minister of finance was a US citizen of Ukrainian origin, Natalia Jaresko, who had worked for the State Department before going into private business. The minister of economy was a Lithuanian, Aïvaras Arbomavitchous, a former basketball champion. The ministry of health was taken by a former Georgian minister of health and labour, Sandro Kvitachvili.

Later, disgraced former Georgian president Mikheil Saakashvili was called in to take charge of the troubled port of Odessa. And Vice President Joe Biden was directly involved in reshuffling the Kiev cabinet as his son, Hunter Biden, was granted a profitable position with the Ukrainian gas company Barisma.

The vehemently anti-Russian thrust of this regime change aroused resistance in the south-eastern parts of the country, largely inhabited by ethnic Russians. Eight days after more than 40 protesters were burned alive in Odessa, the provinces of Lugansk and Donetsk moved to secede in resistance to the coup. The US-installed regime in Kiev then launched a war against the provinces that continued for eight year, killing thousands of civilians. And a referendum then returned Crimea to Russia. The peaceful return of Crimea was obviously vital to preserve Russia's main naval base at Sebastopol from threatened NATO takeover. And since the population of Crimea had never approved the peninsula's transfer to Ukraine by Nikita Khrushchev in 1954, the return was accomplished by a democratic vote, without bloodshed. This was in stark contrast to the detachment of the province of Kosovo from Serbia, accomplished in 1999 by weeks of NATO bombing. But to the United States and most of the West, what was a humanitarian action in Kosovo was an unforgivable aggression in Crimea.

The Oval Office Back Door to NATO

Russia kept warning that NATO enlargement must not encompass Ukraine. Western leaders vacillated between asserting Ukraine's "right" to join whatever alliance it chose and saying it would not happen right away. It was always possible that Ukraine's membership would be vetoed by a NATO member, perhaps France or even Germany.

Meanwhile, on Sept. 1, 2021, Ukraine was adopted by the White House as Washington's special geo-strategic pet. NATO membership was reduced to a belated formality. A Joint Statement on the US-Ukraine Strategic Partnership issued by the White House announced that "Ukraine's success is central to the global struggle between democracy and autocracy" –

Washington's current self-justifying ideological dualism, replacing the Free World versus Communism. It went on to spell out a permanent *casus belli* against Russia:

> "In the 21st century, nations cannot be allowed to redraw borders by force. Russia violated this ground rule in Ukraine. Sovereign states have the right to make their own decisions and choose their own alliances. The United States stands with Ukraine and will continue to work to hold Russia accountable for its aggression. America's support for Ukraine's sovereignty and territorial integrity is unwavering."

The Statement also clearly described Kiev's war against Donbass as a "Russian aggression." And it made this uncompromising assertion: "The United States does not and *will never* recognize Russia's purported annexation of Crimea..." (my emphasis). This is followed by promises to strengthen Ukraine's military capacities, clearly in view of recovery of Donbass and Crimea.

Since 2014, the United States and Britain have surreptitiously transformed Ukraine into a NATO auxiliary, psychologically and militarily turned against Russia. However this looks to us, to Russian leaders this looked increasingly like nothing other than a buildup for an all-out military assault on Russia, Operation Barbarossa all over again. Many of us who tried to "understand Putin" failed to foresee the Russian invasion for the simple reason that we did not believe it to be in the Russian interest. We still don't. But they saw the conflict as inevitable and chose the moment.

Ambiguous Echoes

Putin justified Russia's February 2022 "operation" in Ukraine as necessary to stop genocide in Lugansk and Donetsk. This echoed the US-promoted R2P, Responsibility to Protect doctrine, notably the US/NATO bombing of Yugoslavia, allegedly to prevent "genocide" in Kosovo. In reality, the situation, both legal and especially human, is vastly more dire in Donbass than it ever was in Kosovo. However, in the West, any attempt at comparison of Donbass with Kosovo is denounced as "false equivalence" or what-about-ism.

But the Kosovo war is much more than an analogy with the Russian invasion of Donbass: it is a *cause*. Above all, the Kosovo war made it clear that NATO was no longer a defensive alliance. Rather it had become an offensive force, under US command, that could authorize itself to bomb, invade or destroy any country it chose. The pretext could always be invented: a danger of genocide, a violation of human rights, a leader threatening to "kill his own people". Any dramatic lie would do. With NATO spreading its tentacles, nobody was safe. Libya provided a second example.

Putin's announced goal of "denazification" also might have been expected to ring a bell in the West. But, if anything, it illustrates the fact that "Nazi" does not mean quite the same thing in East and West. In Western countries, Germany or the United States, "Nazi" has come to mean primarily anti-Semitic. Nazi racism applies to Jews, to Roma, perhaps to homosexuals.

But for the Ukrainian Nazis, racism applies to Russians. The racism of the Azov Battalion, which has been incorporated into Ukrainian security forces, armed and trained by the Americans and the British, echoes that of the Nazis: the Russians are a mixed race, partly "Asiatic" due to the Medieval Mongol conquest, whereas the Ukrainians are pure white Europeans.

Some of these fanatics proclaim that their mission is to destroy Russia. In Afghanistan and elsewhere, the United States supported Islamic fanatics, in Kosovo they supported gangsters. Who cares what they think if they fight on our side against the Slavs?

Conflicting War Aims

For Russian leaders, their military "operation" is intended to prevent the Western invasion they fear. They still want to negotiate Ukrainian neutrality. For the Americans, whose strategist Zbigniew Brzezinski boasted of having lured the Russians into the Afghanistan trap (giving them "their Vietnam"), this is a psychological victory in their endless war. The Western world is united as never before in hating Putin. Propaganda and censorship surpass even World War levels. The Russians surely want this "operation" to end soon, as it is costly to them in many ways. The Americans rejected any effort to prevent it, did everything to provoke it, and will extract whatever advantages they can from its continuation.

Volodymyr Zelensky implored the US Congress to give Ukraine more military aid. The aid will keep the war going. Anthony Blinken told NPR that the United States is responding by "denying Russia the technology it needs to modernize its country, to modernize key industries: defence and aerospace, its high-tech sector, energy exploration."

The American war aim is not to spare Ukraine, but to ruin Russia. That takes time. The danger is that the Russians won't be able to end this war, and the Americans will do all they can to keep it going.

First published at https://consortiumnews.com/2022/03/16/diana-johnstone-for-washington-war-never-ends/ and is reproduced with permission of the author.

Europe and NATO Expansion

Frank Blackaby

Frank Blackaby was Director of the Stockholm International Peace Research Institute from 1981 to 1986. First published in 1996, we reprint this commentary for historical context and as an enduring contribution to the analysis of NATO's policy and the dangers it poses.

Introduction

If you say 'Europe' to anyone in Britain these days, it triggers comments on beef, fish, the Conservative Party, and, just possibly, the Inter-Governmental Conference. These are ephemerae. The big issue is as it has always been – how do we make sure that we never again have a great war in Europe? We failed twice this century. It would be wicked to fail again. Could it happen? The way things are going, the answer is – Yes.

Five years ago, peace over the whole of Europe was there for the taking. Western Europe was already a 'security enclave', in this sense: that it was absurd to think that the three old contenders – France, Britain and Germany – would ever again resort to military force to settle disputes between them. Germany had been brought into the Western comity of states: it was no longer an expansionist power. Then from 1985 on, Gorbachev set about removing for good the idea of Soviet expansionism.

It is easy to forget the enormity, and the totality, of that change. Indeed it was not one change: it was about nine changes. The Berlin Wall came down. All Soviet troops left Eastern Germany, and all other Warsaw Pact states as well. The Warsaw Pact was dissolved. The USSR broke up, and two new states were created – Belarus and the Ukraine which stood between Russia and Poland. So Russian troops, withdrawn to their new border, were over 1,000 kilometres away from the new German border. The USSR accepted the reunification of Germany.

There was more. In the five years before its dissolution, the USSR assented to a whole series of Western arms control proposals. It accepted a total zero for all ground-launched ballistic and cruise missiles with ranges from 500km to 5,500km – a proposal the US had put forward in the certainty that the USSR would turn it down. The USSR signed a Treaty on Conventional Forces in Europe which meant far more dismantling and destruction of weapon systems on the Eastern than on the Western side. It agreed to a START Treaty reducing Soviet nuclear weapons much more than those of the US.

Finally, any idea of furthering the worldwide spread of Communism was abandoned. What else could the USSR (and later Russia) have done, to convince the world that it was not an aggressive expansionist power?

A chance

Here then was a chance. For the first time in recorded history there was a chance to create a Europe from the Atlantic to the Urals where the risk of inter-state (not intra-state) war could be reduced down towards zero. This had already happened in Western Europe. Within the region of the European Union security was no longer a military matter. In any dispute between EU members, their relative military capability was irrelevant. Even the fiercest British Eurosceptic, angry at the ban on British beef exports, does not suggest calling the chiefs of staff into Cabinet meetings. The idea of settling disputes within the EU by military means is off the map of political possibility.

This 'security enclave' could have been extended to Eastern Europe. Two things were needed. One was to bring Russia into the comity of nations as an equal partner as had already been done with the Second World War enemy, Germany. The other was to avoid at all costs the creation of a new dividing line in Europe. There should be no going back to the old pattern – an alliance of selected European states against the threat from a European enemy outside the group.

The opportunity was lost. It is not going to be easy to salvage things now.

NATO was clearly not the right body for the new Europe. The North Atlantic Treaty, the Washington Treaty, is a simple, monochrome Treaty. Security organisations fall into two classic categories. There are collective security treaties, which are concerned primarily with conflicts between their members and there are collective defence treaties, which are created to deal with an enemy or enemies outside the group. The Washington Treaty is a collective defence treaty, addressed to an outside threat. It is not – repeat not – a collective security treaty. It has no provisions for dealing with conflicts between its own members. That is one reason why it is so short: it can be printed on one sheet of A4 paper.

Further, NATO was a single-enemy treaty. It had one purpose and one purpose only – to deter the USSR from an attack on Western Europe. It was a military treaty, and nothing else. It had no concern with human rights – there was no question of suspending Greece or Turkey when they were under military dictatorships. It had nothing to do with economic issues. Its purpose was to confront an enemy, the Soviet Union, with military power.

How has it been possible to promote NATO as the dominant security organisation in Europe when the Soviet Union was no longer the enemy? There has been no revision to the Washington Treaty of 1949. It is still for collective defence, and that presumes some enemy. These are some answers to that question.

The promotion of NATO

It soon became clear that, in spite of the loss of the enemy, NATO would remain the United States' chosen instrument of influence in Europe. The US had no intention of allowing the Pan-European Conference on Security and Cooperation in Europe (the CSCE, later the OSCE) to take its place. In NATO, the United States had an undisputed position of leadership. It dominated NATO's decision-making process – for the threat, spoken or unspoken, of US withdrawal from Europe was always there. The CSCE was much too European for American tastes. The USA had (in its view) won the Cold War. Russia was in a chaotic state, so that there was no need to pay much attention to Russian views on any security issue. The general US attitude was: 'We are the masters now'.

In the early period after the fall of the Berlin Wall, some of the Eastern European states, former members of the Warsaw Pact, initially favoured the idea of a pan-European security body. They changed their minds when they understood the US position. Their long period of subjection to Soviet hegemony had left them with one main security obsession: to stay out of any Russian sphere of influence. They wanted a guarantee from the United States that this would not be permitted. The only way they saw of obtaining that guarantee was by becoming members of NATO. For them, NATO was still an organisation for deterring Russia. As one Polish diplomat put it – though not on a diplomatic occasion: 'We are not interested in the fun and games. [He was referring to Partnership for Peace manoeuvres, discussed below.] We just want to make sure that, if there is trouble with Russia, the US marines will be there'.

NATO moved in a somewhat crab-like way to its present position, of accepting the idea that states which were previously members of the Warsaw Pact should be enrolled as full members of NATO. The first move, in 1991, was to establish the North Atlantic Cooperation Council, open to all Central and East European states and, later, to all the successor states of the old USSR. Virtually all the eligible states joined. The Council's function was to provide consultation on defence planning and other military matters. Whether in fact Tajikistan, Kyrgyzstan and Uzbekistan have benefited much from such consultations is perhaps doubtful.

The next step was to develop with some of these states Partnership for Peace (PfP) programmes. It is always as well to be wary when military organisations adopt the word 'Peace'. The US Strategic Air Command had as its motto 'Peace is our Profession' at a time when it was sending B52s with nuclear bombs to loiter near the Soviet border. President Reagan decided to christen the MX Intercontinental Ballistic Missile the 'Peacekeeper' – though most of those writing about US nuclear weapons seem to have jibbed at using this designation.

'Partnership for Peace' programmes might suggest such items as educational programmes in schools designed to encourage children not to hate other nationalities, or the financing of films which show the appalling consequences of modern war. In fact the NATO Partnership for Peace programmes are concerned exclusively with the military: peace was a military matter, to be obtained by military means. So PfP programmes involve such items as joint military exercises, force planning and the development of interoperability. Russia accepted the idea of PfP programmes because it assumed that they were a relatively innocuous substitute for full NATO membership.

Then in January 1994 NATO, at US instigation, decided in principle to admit former Warsaw Pact states as full members of NATO. This epoch-making decision was taken with little public debate in Europe. Europeans were preoccupied with Maastricht and all that. So PfP programmes, instead of being substitutes for NATO membership, were billed as part of the necessary preparations for full membership. The promise of full NATO membership has perhaps been made most explicitly to Poland. In July 1994 President Clinton, no doubt with Polish-American votes in mind, stated before the Polish Parliament: 'Bringing new members into NATO, as I have said many times, is no longer a question of whether, but when and how'.

NATO eventually published a study on enlargement in September 1995. It conveys the message that this enlargement will improve security and stability for all states: the phrase 'security and stability', sometimes varied to read 'stability and security', appears thirty times in the first 11 pages of the paper. The early part of the paper accepts that things have changed, and that there is virtually no risk of 'a re-emergent large-scale military threat'.

It then refers to 'risks to European security which are multi-faceted and multi-directional'. The facets or directions are not specified.

However, the later sections which deal with the modalities of expansion imply that nothing has changed. The conditions of membership are the same. There should be no change in the Treaty – it stays a collective defence Treaty. It is strongly suggested that it would be a good idea for new members to accept the stationing of other allied forces on their territory: '... the stationing of allied forces offers specific military advantages in relation to collective defence'. However, this should be 'neither a condition of membership nor foreclosed as an option'.

On nuclear weapons, 'there is no a priori requirement for the stationing of nuclear weapons on the territory of new members': however, this also is not foreclosed. New members must accept NATO's nuclear weapon doctrine, which still includes possible first use. President Havel of the Czech Republic recently changed the view he previously held, and now allows for the possibility of nuclear weapons on Czech soil. The document states: 'New members should concentrate, in the first instance, on interoperability'. That means that new weapon systems should be bought from manufacturers in NATO countries, not any longer from Russia.

Consequences

This decision – the Eastwards expansion of NATO – seems to have been taken without asking what would happen next. Here three questions are asked. What would happen to relations between Russia and the West? What about the new dividing line between those states which are in NATO and those which are not? If Poland, Hungary, and the Czech Republic join NATO, will they be more secure?

The NATO document on enlargement has a section on relations with Russia. It leaves a vague impression of Russian cooperation, although it does concede that 'Russia has raised concerns with respect to the enlargement process of the Alliance'. This is a massive understatement. The document offers this anodyne reply to those concerns: '. . . The Alliance has made it clear that the enlargement process ... will threaten no-one and contribute to a developing broad European architecture based on true cooperation throughout the whole of Europe, enhancing security and stability for all.'

How does the idea of NATO extension play in Petrozavodsk? Not well. In Russia, unlike Western Europe, the expansion of NATO has been extensively discussed. There is a consensus: it is negative. In 1993 Yevgeniy Primakov, subsequently Foreign Minister, said that if 'the biggest military grouping in the world with colossal offensive potential moved closer to Russia's borders, then this would call for 'a substantial reassessment of the Russian defence concept and a redeployment of armed forces, a change in operative plans'. More recently we have had the speech of the Russian Deputy Defence Minister, Andrei Kokoshin, who in the 1988-92 period had been one of the more prominent advocates of Soviet accommodation with the West. In February 1996 he reminded a Munich audience that the 1990 Treaty on the Final Settlement with Respect to Germany prohibited the stationing of foreign troops in Germany's eastern Länder: the point of the prohibition had been precisely to prevent any Eastward move for NATO. Now NATO was proposing an extension which leap-frogged east Germany and which could bring possibly nuclear weapons and very probably foreign troops even further to the East. Kokoshin said that it would usher in a new era of 'dangerous confrontation'.

In Russia the condemnation of the NATO decision seems universal – in articles, think-tank reports, reactions of political parties and collective statements from the Russian equivalent of the 'great and good'. Opinions differ about what Russia should do if it happens. These are three of the more moderate proposals (the extremists want a military reoccupation of the Baltic republics):

(a) Russia should move to build up a military-political alliance to counter NATO expansion. Belarus would certainly join, and Russia would put great pressure on Ukraine to join as well. President Kuchma of Ukraine has already spoken in Moscow, opposing NATO expansion. So a new, hostile border would be created, between Poland and the states to the East.

(b) Russia should then reintroduce ground-based tactical nuclear weapons to protect the border. Since NATO would then have a formidable superiority in conventional forces, Russia would have to rely much more on nuclear warheads. The decision to withdraw ground-based tactical nuclear weapons was a kind of gentlemen's agreement between Bush, Gorbachev and later Yeltsin. There is no Treaty to prevent their reintroduction. Agreement would be sought to put them on the Belarus-Polish border.

(c) Russia should not ratify either the START II Treaty or the Open Skies Treaty until the idea of an Eastward expansion of NATO is jettisoned.

For the moment Western politicians have put the idea of NATO expansion on the back burner. They hope, by their temporary silence, to be of some help to President Yeltsin's campaign. No doubt President Zyuganov would react more fiercely if the expansion does happen. However, in Russia the hostility to the idea is so widespread that any President would be bound to take some action of some kindl – military as well as political – if the expansion goes ahead.

Which states?

The leading candidates for joining NATO are Poland, Hungary and the Czech Republic; Slovakia is more doubtful. The states at the bottom of the list are the Baltic Republics. This is in some ways a rather odd ranking. In spite of disclaimers, the applicant states are interested in NATO membership for one reason and one reason onlyl – as protection against a resurgent Russia. The Baltic states could claim to be in the greatest need because of their problems with substantial Russian minorities. However, NATO Governments recognise that if these states joined NATO all hell would break loose in Russia: so the Baltic states are at the end of the queue.

So what would happen if Poland, Hungary, and the Czech Republic became full members of NATO? There would be a clear new dividing line in Europe. Further, there would be a *de facto* declaration of spheres of influence. The Western powers would be saying to Russia, in effect: 'We will take those three states into the Western sphere of influence. You can have the rest'. There is no way in which this decision could fail to make a new dividing line in Europe – and a hostile one at that. As a consequence Russia might well put pressure on the Baltic states, on Belarus and on the Ukraine to accept the stationing of Russian forces on their territory.

If Poland, Hungary and the Czech Republic joined NATO, would they in fact be more secure? One argument used a good deal is that these three states are in a 'security vacuum'. This metaphor was extensively used in the debates on NATO expansion in the US Congress. Representative Christopher Smith, for example, described central Europe as a 'no-man's land ... between Germany and Russia'. He cited US political, economic, and security interests on the continent, and argued that NATO could fill a vacuum that would sustain progress made towards democracy and free-market economies in the region.

The vacuum metaphor is not helpful. Vacuums have to be filled by something. The implication is clear: if NATO doesn't move in, Russia will. Why would Russia 'move in', whatever that might mean? It has no common border with the three states any longer. Which would be more profitable for Russial – good relations with these three states, or bad relations? Again, the parallel with Western Europe is useful. Belgium and The Netherlands have common borders with militarily powerful states. They are in a 'security vacuum': NATO does not fill it, since it has no provision for dealing with disputes between Treaty members. For Belgium and The Netherlands the concept of a security vacuum is meaningless: their relations with France and Germany are such that the overwhelming military power of those two states is not relevant.

The sensible course for the three applicant states is to work on developing good relations with Russia, which should not be difficult. If they join NATO, that will simply help to bring about the very thing they fear – a Russia which stops the decline in military spending, starts to build up more powerful military forces, and moves back to military confrontation with the West.

The applicant states should note that the 'NATO guarantee' in Article V of the Washington Treaty is not unequivocal. It does begin by saying that 'an armed attack against one or more [allies] shall be considered an attack against them all'. However, it then goes on to say that each party to the Treaty will assist the ally under attack with 'such action as it deems necessary, including the use of armed force.' There is no unequivocal military commitment. In the US Congressional debate opponents of NATO expansion said that, due to US conventional force reductions in Europe, such expansion would 'create a dangerous gulf between our commitments in Europe and the resources required to meet them'. Representative Hamilton said that 'these conventional force reductions would leave too great a reliance on US strategic nuclear forces to meet the US commitment'. Would the US really threaten a nuclear war in defence of Poland?

However, in spite of this questioning, NATO's military establishment in Brussels has probably already started military contingency planning for three new entrants. It is hard to think of any realistic contingencies – a Russian incursion into Poland through Belarus? – but no doubt military imagination will think of something. There has already been discussion about Poland's flat terrain: does it give more advantage to the invader or the defender? It clearly suggests the use of heavy armour, and that in turn suggests prepositioning. The next stage would be military exercises, which would provoke counter-exercises on the other side. No doubt some of those on the military side in NATO would find it in some ways comforting to be back to business as usual.

For Poland, Hungary and the Czech Republic, the cost of joining NATO, and obtaining such guarantees as Article V provides, is likely to be a much more hostile border to the East. This is a doubtful bargain.

How to get out of this mess

It will not be easy to find a way out of this foolish and unnecessary confrontation with Russia, because neither side will want to lose face. The Americans – fully conscious of their position as the one remaining superpower – have promised NATO membership particularly to Poland. They seem determined to take no notice of anything the Russians say. The Russians, increasingly angry at being treated as some kind of basket case whose views can be totally ignored, would have to do something if this Eastward expansion went ahead. The NATO decision in principle, and the US refusal to accept any modifications which might make the decision more palatable, has already served to increase Russian hostility to the West.

Once it is accepted that NATO's present policy will build up great trouble for the future, it should be possible to find a proposal less provocative to the Russians. For example, NATO and Russia could jointly agree to guarantee existing borders in Central and Eastern Europe. There is the Ukrainian proposal, for a nuclear-weapon-free zone from Sweden in the North to Bulgaria in the South, taking in all the Central and East European states. The range of non-provocative possibilities is wide. The dominant requirements for European security remain – that Russia should be within the structure and not outside it, and that there should be no new dividing line in Europe.

According to Article 10 of the Washington Treaty, any invitation to a new state to join NATO has to have the unanimous agreement of all the existing members. In the debates in the US Congress, the representatives seem not to have noticed this particular clause. They clearly regarded NATO expansion as a matter for the United States alone to decide. Perhaps one or other of the European members of NATO might be prepared to incur US displeasure, and indicate that it might be better to wait for a more comprehensive European security agreement.

Envoi

It is silly to keep repeating that NATO's Eastwards expansion will not create a new dividing line in Europe. Of course it will. It is silly to revert to the old 'fallacy of the last move' that once NATO moves Eastwards, it is the end of the game. It is not. The Russian Government – any Russian Government – will react, militarily as well as politically. Those who draft NATO documents seem to believe that, if they intone the mantra 'security and stability' thirty times, all problems will disappear. They will not. The course is being set for Europe to drift gradually downwards towards Cold War II – 'that stale imposture played on us once again'.

A meeting at Central Hall, Westminster, SW1

(Between St. James' Park Underground Station and Parliament Square)

Friday 13th March 1970 at 7-30 p.m.

Notes & Topics

Speakers include

Gunther Anders
Laurent Schwartz
Members of the International
War Crimes Tribunal

Tran Cong Tuong
Commission for Investigation
of U.S. War Crimes,
Democratic Republic of Vietnam

Ernest Mandel
Conor Cruise O'Brien
Malcom Caldwell
Chairman C.N.D.

Ken Coates
B.R.P.F.

Bill Jones
Chairman I.W.C.

Stan Newens, MP
Chairman M.C.F.

Tony Smythe
General Secretary N.C.C.L.

Raymond Williams
The Spokesman

Honour Bertrand Russell —Carry on his work!

*Organised by The Bertrand Russell Peace Foundation
and The Spokesman, founded by Bertrand Russell*

Partisan Press Ltd. Nottingham England T.U.

Definition

Raymond Williams

*Raymond Williams'
belated centenary
celebrations led us to
revisit his advice in the
early days of The
Spokesman journal. He
was speaking in March
1970, shortly after
Russell's death, at Central
Hall, Westminster, at a
public meeting to 'Honour
Bertrand Russell – Carry
on his Work!'*

Bertrand Russell was an intellectual in politics, not simply an intellectual about politics, which is a very much easier thing to be (studying politics from a distance, a necessary but a different thing). He was an intellectual *in* politics; that is to say a man who was at once and remained over a very long life a working intellectual, who through a succession of world crises never gave up the practice of exacting intellectual work, much of it necessarily lonely, but who at the same time never at any time thought that that work gave him a reason, at certain decisive moments, from going where the political action was. That Russell should have sat in the streets at 90, that he should have done this at that age and at that time, when the whole problem of what it was to be intellectual in this sort of country was in question, was important in a permanent way, quite apart from the degree to which, at particular points, one had to agree with him. It was a definition of a particular role, because in either direction it is so easy to give up. It is easy to say that a particular world situation is so critical that prolonged study and thought, the necessary disciplines of intellectual work, cannot be afforded. Russell never said that. At the same time, it is very easy to say that because intellectual work is necessary there is no time for the business of politics, which is very different, which is rougher, and which, particularly to a man like Russell, involved going beyond the forums he had immediately available to him on the basis of the work he had previously done, and meant going as a man among others in the cause of a popular movement.

I think it is going to be very hard for any

group of people to do, collectively, the kind of work which, in his last years, he was doing; in a sense because his authority was of a very rare kind. Not, I think necessarily, the authority of truth of the beliefs which are at the centre of his intellectual work.

I will say quite frankly that, except in politics, I rarely agreed with him. But in politics I usually did. What was outstanding, I think, was not his rightness, but the authority practically executed over so many years, over what amounted really to several lifetimes in the ordinary sense, the authority of the independent intellectual, even when he was wrong.

The first time I ever had sense of him as an adult, as opposed to the sense I had of him at school and so on, I felt bitterly hostile to him. This was at the time of the preventive war proposal in the late 1940s. At other times I felt neutral, at other times passionately on his side. But the point was that one always knew with this man, and it is a rarer thing than it ought to be, that here was a man whose mind was his own. It was not to be bought, it was not to be pressured. Yet at the same time he knew that his mind could not be only his own, in the reality of social life and in the reality of social crisis. This is the problem that Russell, sometimes magnificently as in the last years, sometimes in error, but always I think as the leading man of his generation who attempted this, continually defined. Where at once your mind is your own, absolutely, and you resist the innumerable pressures of every kind that anybody who does work of this sort is exposed to: pressures of money, which are always available in this society; pressures of loyalty to old friends and comrades, which can often happen when a situation changes; pressures of orthodox public opinion; all the time fear of ridicule, fear of the kind of sneer that comes easily to the Anglo-Saxon mind, that you are going outside your field. All these bids for the man's mind which he has got to resist, but then the one bid for his mind which he cannot resist, which is to put it in the service of something more important even than truth, more important than himself and the preservation of his mind, and this is precisely the crisis Russell faced when he pushed out beyond the highly abstract disciplines in which he had been working to the roughest and most confused and confusing business of social and political reality.

Russell's authority was the authority of the committed independent. That double stress he has earned, and which combined with the reverence due to his age, was an essentially irreplaceable authority. And I don't know really that in that sense one ought to look for replacing it. Because what clearly is involved in the situation I have been describing is the need for the collaboration of independent intellectuals in the sense that Russell was

Definition 43

one; a collaboration, a commitment to a common cause, which is sustainable as a common cause and yet which is not the shabby version of the common cause into which so many intellectuals have again and again found themselves being led. The common cause which is truly open, commonly defined, and yet at the same time which is a common cause and to which commitment is given.

The Chairman has told you that one of Russell's last acts was to found a monthly magazine, *The Spokesman*. I am very glad that this has been done and I was glad to accept an invitation to join its editorial board. I have no authority except as one member of the board among others to speak about its policy, but in line with what I have been previously saying I will say what I think its policy ought to be in the most general terms. I think the situation that we now face in the early 1970s is so complicated that the test will become more severe rather than less. For this reason, on the one hand there is a very visible social crisis of an international kind, an aggressive imperialism which is capable only of being resisted, which has reached the point where it has literally to be fought and where it is fought. That visible crisis is taking place in so many countries of the world, but characteristically away from countries like our own, away from the old imperial countries, leaving those people who are in the old imperial countries in a double situation, having to give very much in the way of support and clarification to that struggle, having to circulate facts, to insist towards their own authorities, and to fight them where necessary, to see that the resources of our people are not enlisted as they have in a sort of tacit default been enlisted, on the wrong side, on the anti-popular side.

There is that commanding crisis which is so visible, and then another one which I think is not very visible at all, something that is happening within this still comparatively peaceful society, something which one cannot predict with any certainty, but which I know in my bones is happening. This is the emergence, the planned emergence, of a new social order, and it is not the social order that Russell or any other progressive man of this century has been talking about. It is the emergence in quite new forms, without obvious kinds of open mass deprivation, the emergence of a controlled society, of a quite new and sophisticated kind, in which very many people will suffer but will suffer in separate groups, in separate ways, on disparate issues, often not recognising in the face of someone else – across the screen as it characteristically will be – a victim of the same process which has made them victims. It will be a process in some ways so indirect, so locked into the apparent normality of this society, so continually fed by a powerful communications system, that day by day the

44   Our Common Security

mind may slip into accepting as normal what no free man ever could accept as normal. And this will be happening at the same time that a visible and a bloody crisis of imperialism is taking place, in the rest of the world, and is part, though in quite different ways, of this thing that is happening to us.

Now I think it will be the business of *The Spokesman* as anything inheriting Russell's role would be bound to do, to carry news of the struggle against imperialism, to carry analyses of it, to carry reports from its leaders as they emerge, because these things are very badly reported indeed in this country. But it will have to do that in ways that don't allow us to become spectators of the struggle for and against imperialism. It will have to be done in ways that continually tie it in to what is happening in this society, in so many sectors: all the way through new conditions of work and the efforts to establish workers' control; through new pressures in education which are of a very severe kind, and the real explanation that it is necessary of the struggle now going on in the universities to maintain a liberal freedom, let alone to extend it. It will have to reach into areas of tension in the society which are still often picked up as personal symptoms, as in some sense matters of some psychological sickness: tensions which may only emerge in that form, but which have forms through which this unprecedented social crisis is taking shape. And it will have to do this not on the one hand and then on the other, which is easy to do. It will have to do it so that it is an attempt at one body of thought.

Even to say that is to recognise that that definition is ideal, that in a sense none of us, even collectively, will know quite enough, will be able to work quite hard enough, will be able to be precise enough. But I think I can say that the people starting *The Spokesman* are going to try. They are introducing this magazine, into what is already a very good and lively press of the Left, with one special emphasis, that they cover a quite broad front of opinion. And I think *The Spokesman* will only in that sense be a spokesman while this remains so, because it is crucially important. The Left has never been more active, yet in a way never more quick to suspicion of each other, and to marking off an indefinite series of fractions which perhaps even Russell's mathematics couldn't have contained. Nevertheless, and I have moved among the fractions and have often become one of the more vulgar, I know perfectly well that within this there is a continual wish to be in touch and to cooperate, to build the kind of front which I think in the 1970s is going to be profoundly necessary. One further emphasis: one which I think comes very near to the sense I have of Russell. Russell was an aristocrat. He had an aristocrat's

Definition

education, he went to what is the first or second most aristocratic college in the first or second most aristocratic university in a profoundly aristocratic society. And when he once said (and I have heard this recording over and over again) 'I will not' — you know, as a form of refusal — one heard that power and background of the aristocrat. The people he used to say 'I will not' to, the people he would write to, whom I wouldn't even know had a letter box, showed the confidence of the aristocrat, and he went in as one of the leading minds of his time, from the centre of a major university, pushed that way all the time.

But still he always insisted that wherever the argument led, and into whatever difficulties of language, in the end the argument only mattered what it came back to the ordinary language of men. It is what I said at the beginning. The intellectual must go where his work leads him, he has no duty higher than that, but when it leads him away from the interests of humanity and away from the language of humanity, something, it may be very hard to find out what, has gone wrong with the work. This attempt by Russell to bring the most rigorous intellectual work back to ordinary issues and ordinary language is the most essential definition I would want to give of *The Spokesman*, because that is what it would earn it its title. That is what would give it some claim other than its succession to be carrying on the work of Bertrand Russell.

Subscribe to The Spokesman
Journal of the Bertrand Russell Peace Foundation

The Spokesman is the journal of the Bertrand Russell Peace Foundation. It features independent journalism on peace and nuclear disarmament, human rights and civil liberties, and contemporary politics.

Subscribe | 3 issues per year | Individuals: £20 UK, £25 RoW
Institutions: £33 UK, £38 Europe, £40 RoW

www.spokesmanbooks.org

Pamela Wood in London in the 1960s

Remember your humanity

Pamela Wood

Pamela Wood shares her memories of working at the Bertrand Russell Peace Foundation during the 1960s.

In July 1962 I was working as a temporary secretary and feeling rather bored. My sister, Shirley Foster, who was a member of the Committee of 100, told me a group of young people who were working for Bertrand Russell were in need of temporary assistance and asked if I was interested. I was, very much so, since I was a great admirer of Lord Russell and had been on numerous anti-nuclear demonstrations – both CND marches and direct action organised by the Committee of 100. So I started to work at 28 Hasker Street, Chelsea, a small house near the one Lord and Lady Russell lived in when they visited London. People working in Hasker Street at the time included Alastair Yule, Ralph Schoenman, Pat Pottle, Nic Johnson and Tom Kinsey. Chris Farley joined the group shortly afterwards. All of them had been involved in the anti-nuclear movement.

The setting up of the Committee of 100 had been an idea suggested to Bertrand Russell by Ralph Schoenman, but by the time I came on the scene preparations were under way to establish a Peace Foundation under Lord Russell's name. So I found myself typing letters for Lord Russell's signature to various eminent people, asking for support for the proposed Foundation. Having joined the team in 1962, it was nine years before I left to do other things, and the Russell Foundation developed in many different ways in those years.

Our place of work moved from Hasker Street to Argyll Mansions, a flat on King's Road, Chelsea and finally to Shavers Place, a small office just off the Haymarket. People came and went but for much of the time I worked for the Foundation Ralph

Schoenman and Chris Farley were Lord Russell's main secretaries. They made frequent visits to his home in North Wales and, acting on his instructions, would draft letters and articles on his behalf as well as conducting the business of the Foundation generally. Packages of papers, including letters for signature, were regularly sent to North Wales by train or posted from a central London post office.

Lord Russell was well known and respected internationally and received communications from all corners of the globe. He gave support to people campaigning for nuclear disarmament, to others who were suffering various forms of discrimination, and to those who were seeking his intervention on behalf of political prisoners. The Commonwealth Heads of Government met in London on a regular basis and he often came to his house in Hasker Street at that time in order to meet leading political figures. If Lord Russell's politics did not find favour with the British or American Governments of the time, the heads of many non-aligned countries were much more open to his views.

One of the first major political events which occurred even before the Foundation was officially set up was the Cuban Missile Crisis. I remember helping to alert the Press to the content of Lord Russell's telegrams to Kennedy and Khrushchev and the replies he received. It was often my job in subsequent years to phone Press organisations and give out statements on behalf of Lord Russell and the Foundation. Inevitably, the British Press was generally hostile. Lord Russell did, of course, describe what took place concerning Cuba in his book *Unarmed Victory*, which also deals with his attempts to mediate between India and China over their border dispute.

Preparations for setting up the Bertrand Russell Peace Foundation were made during the Spring and Summer of 1963 and, as far as I was concerned, these included my typing letters for Lord Russell's signature asking people to act as sponsors. Then, in September, the Press was told of plans to set up both the BRPF and a charitable organisation, the Atlantic Peace Foundation.

A sale of works of art donated to the Foundation was organised at Woburn Abbey as part of an early attempt to raise funds. Indeed, during most of the time I worked for the BRPF money raising was a constant problem and we were often running very low on cash. Money was obviously needed to run an office, to pay permanent members of staff, to cover the costs of printing various publications, and for travel expenses when Lord Russell's representatives travelled abroad. Among many generous donations were paintings by Picasso and Miro. These were, for

Remember your humanity 49

a while, kept in the Shavers Place office – something which I now acknowledge as rather foolhardy. Had anyone known of their presence it would not have been difficult to stage a break-in.

One of the earliest events to be organised by the Foundation was a conference on political prisoners in Iraq, held in a London hotel in February 1965. I remember that one of the participants was Ethel Mannin, the socialist and novelist who had known Lord Russell for many years. Khalid Zaki, a young Iraqi and political refugee who had campaigned against his government, worked at Shavers Place for a while and shared his knowledge of Middle Eastern politics. He was later joined by his brother, Mustapha. Khalid eventually returned to Iraq and was tragically killed by the Iraqi authorities.

While I was at the Foundation a number of people acted as Lord Russell's secretaries or directors of the organisation. They were all bright, capable young men. Many women also worked for the Foundation but, for the most part, in supporting roles – typing letters, articles and Press statements, duplicating material, making phone calls, etc. Some of them were bright, capable young women, but this was the 1960s, before the second wave of feminism really took off. Among the people who worked in the Shavers Place office was a young woman called Janet (whose surname escapes me) who, I believe, was recruited through an employment agency. She was an efficient and conscientious worker but, I think, a little bemused by the whole set-up. Other women who worked from time to time in the office (and who were, perhaps, more committed to its aims) included Sarah Russell (Lord Russell's granddaughter), Edith Schoenman (Ralph's sister), Paula Howard (nee Coleman) and Diane Nair.

Shavers Place was a rather scruffy building – not particularly impressive for foreign visitors. The office was kept as clean as possible by two cleaners, Mrs Payne and her daughter, who worked with us for several years. I doubt it was particularly easy to clean their way around my vertical heap filing system, which was a constant presence on my desk. Unfortunately, every time I tried to lessen its size I was asked to do something 'more important'.

Although Lord Russell and those working with him remained concerned about the danger of nuclear war and the spread of nuclear weapons, the Foundation got involved with many other issues of the day. In November 1963 President Kennedy was assassinated and some time later an American lawyer, Mark Lane, had a meeting with Lord Russell and detailed some of his concerns about flaws in the investigation into the President's death. The Who Killed Kennedy? Committee was set up with headquarters in Shavers Place and Lord Russell and other people associated with the Foundation wrote letters and articles on the subject.

The flat in Argyll Mansions was still in the possession of the Foundation and was often used to accommodate people visiting London. These included Mark Lane and his wife, Anneliese, and his American researcher, Mike Lester. The latter lived in Argyll Mansions for some weeks and spent his time painstakingly analysing what was known about the assassination and going through the Warren Commission Report in meticulous detail. Lord Russell issued a statement when the Report was published, criticising its inadequacies. He was, of course, taken to task for this by much of the Press but one could argue that questions concerning the assassination still need to be answered.

Some of the early Directors of the Foundation resigned after a time. These included Pat Pottle, Charles Ellis and Tom Kinsey. Several people connected with the *New Left Review* were involved for some time. These included Robin Blackburn, Perry Anderson, Alex Cockburn and Fei Ling Davis.

There was quite a spread of views and political affiliations among the people who were drawn into the Foundation's ambit. Sometimes relationships could become explosive and, as with many political organisations, there were clashes of ego, walk-outs and splits.

Among the people who joined in the mid-sixties was Ken Coates, an academic from Nottingham who was involved in the workers' control movement. Although he remained based in Nottingham, he brought with him political contacts such as Pat Jordan and Geoff Coggan, who moved down to London for a time, and, later, Ken Fleet. The two Kens were to remain with the Foundation on a long-term basis.

As the sixties progressed the war in Vietnam began to escalate and Lord Russell increasingly turned his attention in that direction. Articles in the Press and visits to Vietnam made by people connected with the Foundation made clear the suffering of the Vietnamese and the idea of setting up an International War Crimes Tribunal to investigate what had been happening in that country took shape. Large numbers of people in the United States had for some time been campaigning against their Government's policies in Vietnam and, as plans for a Tribunal developed, a number of young Americans came to London to assist in our work. These included Deirdre Griswold and Maryann Weissman from Youth Against War and Fascism, Ernie Tate, and Russell and Susan Stetler. Lord Russell persuaded a number of eminent figures to participate in the Tribunal and the first session was held in London in November 1966. Isaac Deutscher took a major part in the setting up of the Tribunal but unfortunately died in 1967. I have some rather vague memories of the initial session in London and of the formidable presence of both Sartre and de Beauvoir.

For most of the time I worked for the Foundation I was London based, although I did make a few visits to Plas Penrhyn, the Russells' Welsh home. Lord and Lady Russell were very hospitable and I remember afternoon teas, which involved consumption of Red Hackle whisky, as well as the relating of many amusing anecdotes by Lord Russell, often referring back to incidents in his very long life. On one visit to Wales I spent time with Lucy Russell and we became friendly. Lucy was a lovely young woman – intelligent and warm, with a very lively mind. I was very sad, some years later, when I heard of her suicide. For a while, Lucy and her boyfriend moved into a flat I was renting in Hampstead. Unfortunately, we had problems with our landlady and had to move out. So, in 1965 I moved into Argyll Mansions. This meant I grew acquainted with many of the people who stayed there. The kitchen contained a very old electric stove and attempts were made to cook many international dishes on it as people from different countries passed through or stayed for a while.

Among the people who lived in Argyll Mansions were the Stetlers. They first visited in 1966 and returned in 1967 together with their baby son. Morgan was a much-travelled baby during his first year or so. Having got to know the Stetlers, I was impressed with their grasp of international politics. They seemed to be conversant not only with the situation in South East Asia but also had a good deal of knowledge about Latin America. Looking back, I realise a number of the people connected with the Foundation were exceptionally mature and responsible, considering their youth. Being close in age, I was less aware of this at the time, but now that I am pretty ancient I find it more remarkable. I think it reflects well on Lord Russell that, despite his age, he was so interested in what was happening in the world and willing to work with people who were so much his junior. What he brought to the table, of course, was an incredible intellect and a lifetime of experience.

The War Crimes Tribunal developed apace and the Foundation acquired new office space in Rivington Street, East London to house extra people. I never worked in that building and have no clear idea of what the people working there were doing. I do remember that preparations for the Stockholm sessions of the Tribunal were made in both London and Paris. I travelled to Stockholm in 1967 and remember being very moved by the accounts of bombing raids and the subsequent suffering of many

Vietnamese witnesses.

As well as preparing for the Tribunal, people at the Foundation helped set up the Vietnam Solidarity Campaign involving, amongst others, Tariq Ali. There were numbers of demonstrations in the UK against the US involvement in Vietnam in which the VSC participated.

The Tribunal held another session in Roskilde, Denmark, later in 1967 and, in 1968, the Rivington Street office was closed and the numbers of people working for the Foundation diminished. Also in 1968 Ralph Schoenman was barred from entering the UK and he began to work from a New York office. It was probably inevitable that the other Directors of the Foundation at that time decided they could no longer work with him. Lord Russell's own assessment of Ralph's character was published after the former's death in February 1970.

Ken Blackwell, a young Canadian researcher, appeared on the scene in 1966 and eventually he was to put in charge of the Russell Archive, when it was sold to McMaster University of Hamilton, Ontario. Some of the money from this sale made its way into the Foundation's coffers.

After Lord Russell's death the headquarters of the Foundation moved to Nottingham and Shavers Place was vacated. Ownership of the flat at Argyll Mansions had already been given up. I went to work elsewhere early in 1971. By this time Chris Farley and Ken Coates were the principal Directors. Chris was a Director of the Foundation during all the time I worked for it. I was always impressed by what he wrote and aware that he was very careful about backing up his assertions. He was a quiet man but he had a great sense of humour and could be very good company. As for the two Kens, I thought when the Foundation moved to Nottingham it was in very good hands.

I learned a good deal about international politics during the time when I worked for Lord Russell and for the Foundation. I think this has made me less parochial in my attitudes than I might otherwise have been. I wonder how Bertrand Russell would have viewed the world in the twenty-first century. I suspect he would still have been concerned about the spread of nuclear weapons and would also be worried about climate change. Of all the things he wrote, one request he made has remained with me: 'Remember your humanity and forget the rest'.

Common Security

'Common security' can be summed up as the simple but elusive idea that "security is for all of us, or it is for none of us". It is basic common sense but requires a large dose of good sense to be realised. We publish this dossier to encourage such realisation.

For Our Shared Future: Common Security 2022 was launched forty years after publication of the Palme Commission's *Common Security: A Programme for Disarmament*. The new report addresses concerns not included in the original, not least questions of gender and climate change, but in fundamental respects it grapples with the same key question: how to avoid annihilation of humankind in a nuclear inferno?

We re-publish sections from the original Palme Report and two further documents on the concept of nuclear-weapon-free zones. Such zones are an essential component in achieving common security.

**COMMON
SECURITY 2022**

FOR OUR SHARED FUTURE

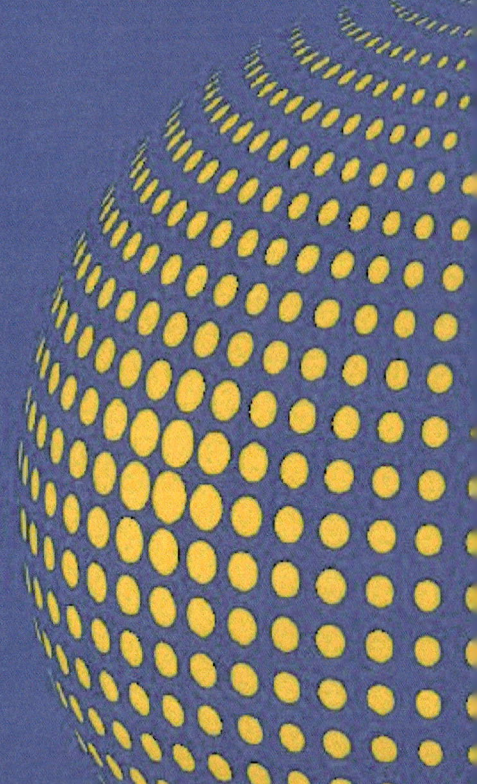

Common Security 2022

For our shared future

Common Security 2022 is the work of the International Trade Union Confederation, the International Peace Bureau and the Olof Palme International Center, together with a 'high-level' commission of experts.

In 1982, the Independent Commission on Disarmament and Security Issues, led by the Swedish Prime Minister Olof Palme, published the report, Common Security: A Programme for Disarmament. *At this time, Cold War tensions and the frightening prospect of nuclear war dominated the international agenda. The report laid bare the horrendous consequences of nuclear conflict, and exposed the fallacy that nuclear deterrence provides security. A nuclear war cannot be won, but would be disastrous for all parties involved. The Commission developed the concept of common security: the idea that cooperation can provide the security that humans crave, where military competition and nuclear deterrence have failed. That ultimately, nations and populations can only feel safe when their counterparts feel safe.*

Common Security 2022: For our shared futures *marks a return to the concepts and proposals of the Palme Commission and situates them in the very dangerous and worrying conditions of the third decade of the twenty-first century. As the new report explains, its "recommendations are indications, or steps forward, in the process of removing the threat of nuclear annihilations and turning around the 'supertanker' of war."*

Foreword

Looking at the news in the morning we are faced with pictures showing the terrible cruelty of war, extreme weather events leaving people homeless, and reports on rising poverty due to the COVID-19 pandemic. The international order, which enables us to prevent wars, stop global warming, fight a pandemic and tackle global challenges, simply does not work well enough. We have to fix it. For our shared future.

In times of acute crisis, there must be those who can look ahead and give a vision of a better future. Forty years ago, the relationship between the superpowers was at rock bottom. The risk of a devastating nuclear war was high. In that situation, an international commission led by Olof Palme presented a report showing that security is something we create together. More and more powerful weapons are not the answer. The concept of common security was established. That way of thinking came to play a role in future negotiations for disarmament and detente.

By taking the concept of Common Security as its starting point, the Common Security 2022 initiative has analysed the world we live in today and some of the great challenges facing humanity. When reading this report, I hope that you will feel an increased optimism about the future. It is possible to make the world better, if we do it together. The idea for this project came from a conversation in February 2020 between myself and Philip Jennings, Co-President of the International Peace Bureau. Common Security 2022 has worked with limited financial and human resources. But because many have shown an enthusiasm and a willingness to contribute their knowledge, we have created this document together. The International Trade Union Confederation, the International Peace Bureau and the Olof Palme International Center are three organisations different in nature, but we all share a vision of a more peaceful world. When starting this journey, little did we know of the situation we would find ourselves in when presenting this report. Some may say it is naïve to even talk about peace, disarmament and common security when the world is on the brink of a new world war. But, on the contrary, now more than ever, we need a stronger discourse for peace.

I would like to extend a deep thank you to all the members of our High-Level Advisory Commission for the time you have spent attending meetings and providing input to the report. The Commission consists of a highly qualified and hugely experienced group of people from all over the world. The collective knowledge within the Commission is what makes this initiative unique. I would also like to thank everyone who participated in the Common Security 2022 webinar series. The webinars provided us with valuable expertise and insights that are reflected here in the report. To my fellow Steering Committee members, thank you for your time, dedication and engagement. But there are two people I would like to give an extra heartfelt thanks to: Björn Lindh, our coordinator, and Clare Santry, our editor. Without the two of you we would never have pulled this off.

This initiative does not end with the presentation of this report. Rather, it should be seen as the beginning of work that must continue for a long time to come. Our world is in danger, but together we can build our common security.

Anna Sundström
Secretary General, Olof Palme International Center

Introduction

The world stands at a crossroads. It is faced with a choice between an existence based on confrontation and aggression or one to be rooted in a transformative peace agenda and common security. In 2022, humanity faces the existential threats of nuclear war, climate change and pandemics. This is compounded by a toxic mix of inequality, extremism, nationalism, gender violence, and shrinking democratic space. How humanity responds to these threats will decide our very survival.

This year marks the 40th anniversary of Olof Palme's Independent Commission on Disarmament and Security Issues. The Commission presented its report in 1982, at the height of the Cold War, and the Commission developed the concept of Common Security – the idea that nations and populations can only feel safe when their counterparts feel safe. Palme's Commission established a number of 'principles' – including that all nations have a right to security, that military force is not a legitimate means for resolving disputes between nations, and that reductions and limits on arms are necessary for mutual security.[1] In January 2022 the leaders of the five permanent members of the UN Security Council jointly stated that a nuclear war cannot be won and must never be fought.[2] This echoed the declaration by US President Ronald Reagan and the Soviet General Secretary Mikhail Gorbachev at their Geneva Summit Meeting in 1985.[3]

Our new Common Security 2022 report comes at a time when the international order faces severe challenges. A devastating war is raging in Europe and unceasing conflicts continue to plague people in far too many places. We are witnessing a global crisis marked by the inability to stop climate change, a patchy and unequal global approach to the COVID-19 pandemic, and a long list of conflicts where the international community has failed in its response. Even before the start of the COVID-19 pandemic more than six out of seven people worldwide felt insecure.[4]

Our common systems and structures – needed to provide security, combat poverty and inequality and prevent human suffering – are inadequate, and frequently ignored or violated. The future of humanity depends on us fixing the struggling global order. If we fail to repair our common systems, we will also fail in our fight against the climate crisis and future pandemics.

The global security system is teetering on the edge. As the UN Secretary-General's report *Our Common Agenda* says: "Humanity faces a stark and urgent choice: breakdown or breakthrough."⁵

This breakdown should serve as a wake-up call for the world.

Since the Palme Commission there have been multiple wars and acts of military aggression that show a blatant disregard for international law, such as in Iraq, Yemen and most recently in Ukraine.

The Russian invasion of Ukraine in February 2022, while this report was being finalised, represents a catastrophic breakdown in common security. It has resulted in a horrific loss of life, millions of refugees and displaced people, and global economic shockwaves. It is a terrible reminder of the fragility of peace. A ceasefire and peace settlement between Ukraine and Russia should be reached without delay in the interests of the Ukrainian and Russian peoples.

This breakdown in security is a reminder of the importance of international cooperation and respect for international law. The current system needs to be overhauled to prevent war and meet the common security interests of all states.

There is an ongoing militarisation in the world, with rapid increases in military spending accompanied by nuclear threats. But nuclear and military deterrence strategies have categorically failed to achieve peace and stability. It is time for a renewal of the global security system, based on common security principles. Now more than ever, we need a strong and efficient multilateral system for peace and security. To turn the tide, we must:

• Reaffirm the UN Charter based on the rights and obligations of "we the peoples".⁶ International cooperation and respect for international law must be fundamental to all states.
• Revitalise and implement the call by the UN Secretary General for a worldwide ceasefire as the starting point for peace processes in different regions of the world.
• Reinforce respect for International Humanitarian Law as a matter of urgency, given the increasing harm to civilians in recent conflicts.
• Realise that global peace and security are created jointly – that when your counterpart is not secure, you will not be secure either. There must be respect for the UN Charter's prohibition against the use of force and the inviolability

of borders.[7]
- Recognise that the threat of nuclear war and climate change are both existential threats to humanity.
- Strengthen trust between states and peoples, so that countries with different systems, cultures, religions and ideologies can work together on global challenges.
- Build a world order based on human needs. There is no development without peace, nor peace without development. And neither is possible without respect for human rights.
- Ensure inclusive governance at all levels in society, to safeguard democratic principles and the inclusion of women, young people and minorities.

Forty years on from the original Palme Commission, the challenges of our interdependent global society demand, more than ever, collaboration and partnership rather than isolation and distrust. Common Security is about human beings, not just nations. Now, in 2022, it is time to consider whether Common Security can help bring us back from the brink.

Common Security 2022: The Principles

Although the world is now in a very different place to forty years ago, the Common Security 2022 project looked back to see whether the original concept of Common Security endured, and how it could be adjusted to be relevant and pertinent to our times. With that in mind, in this report we established six new principles for Common Security. These principles retain the spirit of Palme's Commission but reflect the new threats and complexities of the modern world.

1. All people have the right to human security: freedom from fear and freedom from want.
2. Building trust between nations and peoples is fundamental to peaceful and sustainable human existence.
3. There can be no common security without nuclear disarmament, strong limitations on conventional weapons and reduced military expenditure.
4. Global and regional cooperation, multilateralism and the rule of law are crucial to tackling many of the world's challenges.
5. Dialogue, conflict prevention and confidence-building measures must replace aggression and military force as a means of resolving disputes.
6. Better regulation, international law and responsible governance also need to be extended to cover new military technologies, such as in the realms of cyberspace, outer space and "artificial intelligence".

A Call to Action

The need to move away from the idea of nuclear deterrence as a foundation of international security is more urgent than ever. The nuclear threats used by nations reveal the flimsy basis upon which nuclear deterrence is supposed to work. Humanity will not survive a nuclear war, nor can we prepare for or mitigate the consequences of nuclear war. So an alternative path must be found. A positive and cooperative approach to security must be developed, as a means to making people and governments feel secure. Common security is the alternative to nuclear competition and the threat of mass destruction.

The COVID-19 pandemic has demonstrated that without international cooperation, a global crisis is very difficult to address. Incremental change is not sufficient to save humanity. Action at government level needs to be complemented by action at the level of local communities. A new social contract must be established, and a new dialogue of peace should replace the narrative of militarisation and competition. This approach should place accountability, verification, and transparency at its heart.

Common Security requires action from not just governments but also from national parliaments and from civil society – including from NGOs, social justice and peace movements, faith communities, women's and youth movements, and trade unions. In addition, the corporate sector has a responsibility to respect human rights and to contribute to human security, as stipulated by the UN's *Guiding Principles on Business and Human Rights*.[8]

There is an urgent need for institutions and laws that engage and involve citizens and not only policy- and decision-makers, in cross-border discussions, fairer trade, climate solutions, reducing inequality, and peace and confidence building. Civil society must act as a watchdog, a motivating force, and a counterweight to political posturing – with the support of the verification and trust-building measures included in existing and new treaties. Furthermore, non-governmental organisations must play an active role in advocacy work and raising awareness – not just on common security, but also on militarisation, just conversion and beyond. Dialogue at diplomatic levels should also involve organised civil society – both alongside and separate from government dialogue.

The threat of war and its consequences have not diminished over the years. But political will, people power, and a collective attitude can lead to change. There is still time to be innovative and ambitious in reframing security and reimagining our world.

Recommendations

The Common Security 2022 recommendations are indications, or steps forward, in the process of removing the threat of nuclear annihilation and turning around the 'supertanker' of war. They are practical steps, but also set out a vision for a better, safer world. They aim to motivate public opinion and have a positive impact on policy- and decision-makers about what is necessary and achievable. It is for others to take these proposals forward – in particular the UN with a broader engagement of civil society rather than just of governments. The recommendations in this report are in no way complete or the last word. There is still much work to do to realise Olof Palme's vision of common security.

These recommendations originate from the global experts who took part in the Common Security 2022 Project. The recommendations should be spread through representative organisations and forums – such as the UN Social Summit, the World Social Forum and World Economic Forum, the Organisation for Security and Co-operation in Europe (OSCE), the Organisation for Economic Co-operation and Development (OECD), the UN Conference on Disarmament (CD), the Munich Security Conference, and the Peace and Security Council of the African Union.

The recommendations will also be disseminated via social and traditional media communications, through mass organisations and civil society such as peace and environmental activists, faith communities, trade unions and the women's, youth and civil rights/ racial justice movements. The recommendations are focused on four main areas:

1. Strengthen the Global Architecture for Peace
2. A New Peace Dividend – Disarmament and Development
3. Revitalised Nuclear Arms Control and Disarmament
4. New Military Technologies and Outer Space Weapons

1. Strengthen the Global Architecture for Peace

The multilateral system has come under increasing strain in recent years. There is an urgent need to strengthen the structures that uphold peace and that prevent and manage conflict. Multilateralism must also confront the critical challenge of climate change and of creating fit for purpose global architecture for pandemic preparedness and response.

1.1 Encourage regional bodies, such as the African Union, the Community of Latin American and Caribbean States (CELAC), the South Asian Association for Regional Cooperation (SAARC), the Gulf Cooperation Council, and the Association of Southeast Asian Nations

(ASEAN) to develop frameworks that incorporate the principles of common security, and to build structures that can mediate and build confidence between antagonistic sides. Deter the creation of new military alliances and reassess existing military alliances – using cooperation based on common security as an alternative.

1.2 Establish or renew global and regional peace architecture, building on the model of the Organisation for Security and Co-operation in Europe (OSCE). Hold a Helsinki II process in 2025 – 50 years after the first Helsinki agreement laid the foundations for the OSCE and proposed that human rights and freedom of expression should be the foundation of peace.

1.3 Support the immediate resumption of strategic stability talks between the USA and Russia and the resumption of strategic dialogue between the USA and China, with a view to the final elimination of all weapons of mass destruction.

1.4 Integrate climate-related security risks into United Nations conflict-prevention strategies. Commit to the sharing of green technologies, the redistribution of military resources for tackling the climate threat, and the promotion of alternative solutions to environmental problems. Ensure justice for those nations most affected by climate change – through reparations, relocation, and support for climate-resistant infrastructure.

1.5 Establish regular UN Peace Conferences on the basis of the UN report *Our Common Agenda*, following the model of the United Nations Framework Convention on Climate Change (UNFCCC) Conference of the Parties (COP). Hold the Peace Conferences every three years to review progress on arms control treaties, address the peace dialogue gap and provide scope for intergovernmental agreements. Bring civil society into the centre of the discussions, just as the tripartite International Labour Organization (ILO) is able to do in the way it works.

1.6 Expand the mandate and resources of the UN Peacebuilding Fund and Commission to be used in transnational dialogue processes, people-to-people contact and collaboration, and democratic mobilisation. Continue the Fund's strong focus on women-centred peacebuilding solutions. Use the Fund to increase the number of multi-disciplinary, multi-cultural and multi-faith peace universities, colleges and Congresses ensuring that they are present in regions and nations at risk of conflict. These institutions give younger generations the knowledge, skills and tools to create the conditions and institutions for practical conflict resolution and peace.

1.7 Strengthen the international agenda for Women, Peace and Security by setting a 50 per cent goal for women's participation at all levels of international peace and security undertakings.

1.8 Reform the UN to give more power and authority to the General Assembly – particularly on security matters – to avoid individual members paralysing the whole UN common security system.

2. A New Peace Dividend – Disarmament and Development

The international community needs to find a way to create a vested interest in peace, with the goal of general and complete disarmament. This also means finding innovative ways to utilise equipment and expertise for peaceful purposes and to support the transition of military personnel to non-military professions – the idea of "transforming weapons into windfarms".[9] More than simply a financial benefit, this new peace dividend should help tackle the causes of conflict and fear – such as climate change, inequality, migration, scarce resources, and pandemics.

2.1. Strengthen international law and revitalise treaties in the area of disarmament, arms control, non-proliferation and the arms trade – particularly the Arms Trade Treaty (ATT). Establish strong international rules on the export and use of small arms and light weapons, breaches of International Humanitarian Law, violent crime and terrorism. Adopt a political declaration against the use of explosive weapons in populated areas and strengthen existing commitments, such as the 'Safe Schools Declaration' that protects schools and universities from attack.

2.2. Convene a special UN General Assembly for disarmament in 2023/2024 to set a global commitment to reduce military expenditure by two per cent per year. Set a global ambition to abolish nuclear weapons to free-up more than USD 72 billion annually.[10]

2.3. Use the reduction in military spending to generate a 'global peace dividend' to fund the UN Sustainable Development Goals, UN peacebuilding, and a just transition to climate friendly jobs. Establish a UN 'just conversion' institution and aim to create 575 million new jobs by 2030 – through converting jobs and technology in the weapons industry into environmental and health innovation, and vaccines and treatments. Reduce spending on military personnel by creating civil service options as an alternative to military service.

2.4. Invest in human security by creating a New Social Contract that tackles inequality and builds a more inclusive, resilient and peaceful society. Forge the new social contract by implementing the 2019 Centenary Declaration of the ILO; holding a World Social Summit in 2025; setting-up a Global Social Protection Fund; creating a universal floor of workers' rights; establishing a multilateral binding treaty that imposes human rights due diligence on companies across supply chains, and regularise more than one billion informal and platform jobs. Reinforce the fight against inequality by establishing a global commission and regulatory instrument focusing on transnational tax levels and systems, illicit financial flows, and national social security systems and taxation.

3. Revitalised Nuclear Arms Control and Disarmament

The recognition that a nuclear war cannot be won and must never be fought demands the complete abolition of nuclear weapons. The first steps in the process of comprehensive nuclear disarmament must be taken immediately and in good faith. The imperative to prevent the catastrophic humanitarian consequences of a nuclear war should unify the international community and underscore the urgency for progress.

3.1 Reinstate arms control treaties, particularly regarding nuclear weapons and their delivery systems, for example the Intermediate-Range Nuclear Forces Treaty (INF). As a first step, a moratorium on a deployment of the INF land-based systems in Europe should be introduced. Parties to the Nuclear Non-Proliferation Treaty (NPT) must urgently develop and present concrete, time-bound, and transparent plans of how they intend to implement their obligation to nuclear disarmament. Ensure that the Comprehensive Nuclear Test-Ban-Treaty (CTBT) enters into legal force. Negotiations should begin on a treaty prohibiting any additional production of fissile materials for use in nuclear weapons. Reinstate and develop confidence-building measures, such as the Open Skies Treaty.

3.2 States are encouraged to sign and ratify the Treaty on the Prohibition of Nuclear Weapons (TPNW). Nuclear-armed states should engage with the treaty and send observers to the Meeting of States Parties.

3.3 Resume with urgency nuclear arms reductions, with a view to achieving the elimination of all weapons of mass destruction. Prioritise the states that possess the most nuclear warheads, but include all nuclear-armed states from the start. Cease the development of new nuclear weapons, as well as the modernisation and upgrading of nuclear arsenals. Nuclear-armed states, and states under extended nuclear deterrent arrangements, should engage with non-nuclear weapon states in a serious process to discuss how to move away from the nuclear deterrence paradigm, and to develop alternative security approaches and policies.

3.4 All nuclear-weapon states must establish a firm 'no first use' policy.

3.5 Revisit the idea of establishing nuclear-weapon-free-zones, particularly in the Middle East/West Asia, Northeast Asia, and in Europe.

3.6 The Joint Comprehensive Plan of Action (JCPOA), known commonly as the Iran nuclear deal, must be fully reinstated and faithfully implemented by all signatories.[11]

3.7 States that carried out nuclear testing must provide immediate victim assistance and environmental remediation, particularly to indigenous communities.

4. New Military Technologies and Outer Space Weapons
The digital revolution gives us information and communication technologies that make our lives easier, but it also creates new risks. Modern military weapons systems are being developed which have a profound impact on humanity and raise serious legal and ethical questions. New weapons technologies need to be regulated or prohibited.

4.1 Ban cyber attacks on nuclear command and control systems, accompanied by a disentanglement of conventional and nuclear weapon command and control systems.

4.2 Prohibit autonomous weapons systems, to ensure that humans keep control over weapons and armed conflict.

4.3 Prohibit automated nuclear weapons command and control systems.

4.4 Prohibit attacks on space-based early warning satellites and early warning communications systems.

4.5 Strengthen the Outer Space Treaty and establish a new culture of responsible space governance to prevent further militarisation of the domain. Reinforce international space law to safeguard its use for peaceful purposes and for the benefit of all humanity.

4.6 Limit hypersonic missiles, and create a timeframe for banning these weapons.

The Olof Palme Commission and the Concept of Common Security

In the early 1980s, the Independent Commission on Disarmament and Security Issues, led by the Swedish Prime Minister Olof Palme, developed the concept of Common Security: the idea that cooperation is the only way to provide the security that humans crave, where military competition and nuclear deterrence have failed. Palme's premise also asserted that fewer weapons, rather than more weapons, leads to increased security for all. As Sweden's Minister for EU Affairs, Hans Dahlgren, who worked for the Palme Commission, says "we cannot achieve sustainable security with an adversary by threatening his life".[12]

The Independent Commission was established in 1980. It consisted of

14 high-profile individuals from around the world, including from the United States and the Soviet Union. The members were predominantly former politicians and diplomats. All bar one – the former Prime Minister of Norway, Gro Harlem Brundtland – were men. Two years later, following extensive meetings and research, the Commission published the report, *Common Security: A Programme for Disarmament*. The report laid bare the horrendous consequences of nuclear conflict, and exposed the fallacy that nuclear deterrence provides security. As the report stated, ''International Security must rest on a commitment to joint survival rather than a threat of mutual destruction.''[13]

At the time of Palme's Commission, Cold War tensions and the frightening prospect of nuclear war dominated the international agenda. The principles and recommendations proposed in the report reflected the dominant global dynamic at the time: the clash of two superpowers – the Soviet Union and the USA. For this reason, the Palme Commission was almost entirely focused on nation states and the overriding threat from national militaries.

The recommendations of the Palme Commission were wide ranging. They included: reductions and qualitative limitations of nuclear forces; a nuclear-weapon-free zone in Europe; a ban on anti-satellite systems; universal adherence to the Non-Proliferation Treaty; and conversion of a large proportion of military, scientific and technological efforts to civilian purposes.[14]

The concept of Common Security, developed by the Palme Commission, proved significant in the years following the publication of the report. The President of the Soviet Union, Mikhail Gorbachev, cited the importance of the idea of Common Security in March 1986 – marking what was to be the start of the end of the Cold War.[15] Yet, despite the disarmament moves of the 1980s, the ideas and recommendations of the Palme Commission have, for the most part, not been adhered to or acted upon.

The concerns and focus of the original report have a disturbing resonance in 2022. The Cold War of the 1980s, the nuclear threat and the risk of major power conflict have renewed relevance in today's global situation. But the idea of security must be broadened beyond nation states to include all people. Human beings desire, and have a right to, security. Forty years on from the Palme Commission, the world also faces new existential threats that pay no heed to national borders – such as climate change and pandemics.

Common Security Risks Today

In 2022 human existence faces both old and new threats and challenges. There are also issues that were apparent forty years ago, but have become more pronounced in recent years. The Russian invasion of Ukraine has been accompanied by a threat of nuclear weapons use, which is an alarming echo of the Cold War rhetoric. But, there are also other challenges facing humanity today. The climate crisis is an enormous existential risk for humankind. Meanwhile, inequality and rising authoritarianism have a corrosive and insidious effect on global society. Today's common security risks can be categorised under six broad themes:

Challenges to Multilateralism in a Multipolar World

In 1982, the world was divided into two camps; but since the end of the Cold War new powers have come onto the world's stage with differentiated interests and alliances. Yet – despite these geopolitical realignments – strategic competition and power struggles between nations continue unabated. Borders have shifted and alliances have waxed and waned; but conflict and violence remain constant. According to the Heidelberg Institute for International Conflict Research, the number of full-scale wars increased from 15 to 21 between 2019 and 2020.[16]

In his address to mark the 75th anniversary of the UN General Assembly, the UN Secretary General warned that, "conventional wars are growing more entrenched and difficult to resolve. Geopolitical tensions are escalating. The threat of nuclear proliferation and confrontation has returned".[17]

The critical challenges facing the world demand a renewed commitment to strategic cooperation through multilateralism and institution building. But instead the world has entered a new era of strategic confrontation and competition. The inviolability of borders and respect for the territorial integrity of states is undermined and disregarded. The Russian invasion of Ukraine is one example of a flagrant violation of the UN Charter, upon which multilateralism rests. The validity of the international rules-based system still stands, but it is increasingly in crisis, with the rules being ignored and violated.

Respect for the core principles of international humanitarian law is increasingly under threat, as witnessed in recent conflicts such as Iraq, Palestine/Israel, Yemen, Syria, and Ukraine. These conflicts have seen horrific civilian casualties, the use of explosive weapons in densely populated areas and the deliberate targeting of schools, hospitals and vital civilian infrastructure, such as water and energy supplies.

All too often, military solutions are the default response to global disputes. The role of the 'military-industrial complex' – when an element of the economy has inappropriate political influence – needs to be addressed to make common security viable. While any profit and wealth resulting from war and destruction is morally abhorrent, governments must, at the very least, ensure that military expenditure does not attain a self-sustaining and self-reproducing power over political decision-making. Moreover, the huge investment in military personnel around the world is a catastrophic waste of capabilities. Globally, the United States, China, North Korea and Russia employ the largest number of people in the arms industry. Fifty per cent of the military budget of NATO countries is spent on personnel.[18]

Gender equality in the quest for peace and security was a relatively unexplored topic by the Palme Commission. Yet, women, men, boys and girls are differently affected by security crises. Women and children are often the first signifiers of a humanitarian crisis. Statistics show that when women are at the negotiating table, peace agreements are more likely to last 15 years or longer.[19] But between 1992 and 2019 women constituted, on average, just 13 per cent of negotiators. Moreover, just 6 per cent of signatories in major peace processes around the world were women.[20]

In an increasingly multipolar world, regional conflicts and emergencies frequently spill over into the global arena. Diplomacy and open channels of communication between countries are more vital than ever – as rifts between the USA/China and the USA/Russia demonstrate. Taiwan and the South China Sea are flash points for the rivalry between the USA and China, where a mishap between warships or warplanes could have terrible consequences. Ukraine has turned, with horrible consequences, into an epicentre of confrontation between Russia and USA/NATO.

In the twenty-first century, populations and nations cannot expect to isolate themselves from the rest of the world in order to live securely. It is clear that global issues cannot be solved by individual nations, only by multilateral cooperation among them. Yet, many countries do not seek this cooperation, and this national egoism threatens our common future.

The Palme Commission sought to empower the UN for the purposes of peace. Today, the UN's role in peacekeeping and peacebuilding is one of the most visible examples of international cooperation. But the authority of, and trust in, the United Nations as the prime global governance body is increasingly undermined and challenged.

Today's geopolitical confrontation is being waged on many fronts. So-called 'hybrid warfare' spans economics, trade, political philosophy, democratic principles, technology and military power. The use of disinformation, proxies and cyber attacks blur the line between combatants and civilians, and engender distrust between nations and peoples.

An estimated two billion people live in conflict-affected countries and in 2020 there were 56 State-based conflicts – a record number.[21] There are also 'frozen' conflicts that come in different forms. Sometimes it is where a past conflict has not found a stable resolution, for example there has never been a formal peace settlement ending the Korean War. In other cases it is where land or sea is disputed or occupied – examples of this include Western Sahara, Georgian territories, Nagorno-Karabakh, and Transnistria. While some of these conflicts are between individual states, others are civil wars, insurgencies and guerrilla actions – such as in central India. Several are, in part, proxy conflicts where the actual combatants are influenced by, supplied by, or acting at the behest of global or regional powers. Israel's occupation of Palestinian Territory is more complex still, although there are elements of several typologies involved. Other unresolved conflicts, for example between India and Pakistan, involve states that have acquired nuclear weapons.

A multipolar world requires common security to be promoted through multilateralism. This multilateralism needs to be sensitive, and adapted, to different conflicts and different regions.

Global Warming and Climate Crisis

In addition to nuclear weapons, the world is facing a new existential threat in the form of the climate crisis. Climate-related risks have far-reaching implications for the health of humanity and the planet. If unaddressed, climate change will cast a major shadow over humanity's survival.

Climate change is already affecting the lives of people around the world. Global temperature rises are fuelling droughts and wildfires. July 2021 was the hottest month ever recorded, and the last decade is the hottest since records began.[22] Extreme weather, such as storms and floods, threaten people's lives and livelihoods and expose millions of people to acute food and water insecurity, particularly in Africa, Asia, Central and South America, on Small Island Developing States (SIDS) and in the Arctic.[23]

There are many other major environmental challenges that are linked to the climate crisis. Biodiversity and habitat loss, and the impoverishment of those who once were able to subsist on the land, are just some of the examples. Other effects of climate change, such as rising sea levels, will take longer to unfold.

Gendered divisions of labour mean women are often responsible for collecting water and sourcing food and fuel, particularly in rural areas. This leaves women disproportionately vulnerable to changes in the availability of natural resources. Yet, women are consistently disadvantaged in terms of land ownership and control over these resources. Excluding women from natural resource management and climate change mitigation strategies is patently wrong and also a missed opportunity. As the Georgetown Institute for Women, Peace and Security says: "Where women can overcome structural barriers to their participation, they are uniquely positioned to contribute to sustainable natural resource management, climate-resilient communities, and enhanced peace and stability."[24]

When environmental problems – such as lack of water – become too big, then the result is social unrest, conflict and war. There is an alarming overlap between ecological degradation and conflict. Of the 15 countries facing the worst ecological threats in the world, 11 are currently in conflict. Meanwhile, by the end of 2020 conflict had forcibly displaced 34 million people from their home nations. Of this total, 68 per cent came from the 30 countries described as 'ecological hotspots' by the Institute for Economics and Peace.[25]

Climate change is a risk multiplier for every existing vulnerability and tension. Climate change fosters inequality, increases insecurity, destabilises existing relationships, fuels forced migration, and intensifies competition for key and scarce resources.

However, the activism and determination of the climate change movement over the past few years has united populations and nations. There is now a momentum for climate cooperation, which is driven by people power. Climate change offers a unique opportunity for rallying collective action in the pursuit of global peace.

Inequality

The Olof Palme Commission met between 1980 and 1982. During the 1980s and after, neoliberal globalisation became the dominant economic model. Individualism and profit maximisation, coupled with minimal investment in jobs, wages and social security, have left the world with a ticking time bomb of critical inequality.

A century ago the ILO was created on the premise that "universal and lasting peace can be established only if it is based upon social justice".[26] Similarly, the Palme Commission warned that economic inequality, poverty and deprivation were major threats to security, and that "peace and prosperity are two sides of the same coin".[27] Forty years later, rising income inequality has been blamed for increasingly polarised politics, and the ascendance of populism and nationalism.

All too often, political conflict spirals into violence and war. Social unrest, exclusion and alienation also lead to violence outside of conflict areas, such as urban violence, the rise in power of organised crime, and domestic violence. The presence of conflict also leads to an increased likelihood of terrorism. The Institute for Economics and Peace found that 97.6 per cent of deaths from terrorism, in 2020, occurred in countries affected by conflict and that "as the intensity of conflict increases, so does the lethality of terrorist actions. Terrorist attacks in conflict countries are more than six times deadlier than attacks in peaceful countries."[28]

The discrimination and marginalisation evident across the globe today are symptoms of an extremely unequal world; that exacerbates the differences among us. Nearly half of the world's population – 3.4 billion people – survives on less than $5.50 a day. Meanwhile, women around the world earn 24 per cent less than men and own 50 per cent less wealth.[29] Global income inequality is increasing, according to the UN Special Rapporteur on Extreme Poverty and Human Rights. Since 1980, the top 10 per cent of earners have held half of the world's income; whilst the top one per cent of earners increased their share from 16 per cent in 1980 to 22 per cent in 2000. Latin America and the Middle East are the world's most unequal regions, with the top 10 per cent of earners capturing 54 and 56 per cent, respectively, of the average national income.[30]

Inequality between and within nations masks a major persistent inequality – gender. The inequality faced by women in many countries often involves prioritising care for their families and concentrates them in occupations which are, partly in consequence, under-funded and therefore reproduce gender inequality in income. This vicious cycle of discrimination – and the persistent problem of gender-based violence in workplaces, homes and public – results in the exclusion of women from decision-making roles in society, including over issues of peace and war.[31] It is therefore unsurprising that while the women's movement is a leading force for peace, decisions on military expenditure, foreign policy and war are made in male-dominated environments.

Since the Palme Commission, there has been progress in tackling some aspects of inequality. In 2019, the global primary school attendance rate reached 87 per cent, while the number of out-of-school children has declined by more than 40 per cent over the past two decades.[32] However, in 2020 the World Bank recorded a rise in extreme poverty, reversing a 20-year steady decline.[33] The COVID-19 pandemic, climate change, and armed conflict are among the forces driving this backward slide.

Common Security 2022

Current and future pandemics

COVID-19 has brutally underlined that the world is more interdependent than ever, and that a pandemic threat will know no national boundaries. As the climate becomes more degraded and the biosphere changes, there will likely be more frequent and more serious pandemics.

With the emergence of COVID-19, the scientific community responded effectively and speedily to create vaccines and treatments. But problems arose from the state of the world's trading arrangements, including the protection of intellectual property rights founded on public investment and in a state of emergency. Underfunded health services and social protection systems, coupled with growing health inequality, prevented vaccine equity and exposed the weakness in pandemic preparedness, and prevention. Global society appears increasingly vulnerable to future pandemics.

Inequality has been exacerbated by COVID-19. According to Oxfam International, the world's 10 richest men doubled their fortunes during the global pandemic. Meanwhile the organisation projects that over 160 million people were pushed into poverty by the pandemic.[34] Inequalities that existed before COVID-19 – in terms of income and access to education, health and vaccines – also resulted in the faster reopening of ordinary life and economic activity in some countries compared to others. Universal social protection and the fair distribution of economic growth are vital for building future resilience.

The pandemic, and disagreements over the response to COVID-19, also fuelled divisions and conflict. The Institute for Economics and Peace found that civil unrest rose during the pandemic, with over 5,000 pandemic-related violent events recorded between January 2020 and April 2021.[35]

Women's employment has been disproportionately affected by the pandemic. This is particularly notable in upper-middle-income countries, where "women's employment-to-population ratio in 2022 is projected to be 1.8 percentage points below its 2019 level, versus a gap of only 1.6 percentage points for men, despite women having an employment rate 16 percentage points below that of men to start with".[36] Other repercussions of the COVID-19 pandemic are still being assessed. But the ILO is projecting a working-hour deficit of 52 million full-time jobs in 2022. Meanwhile, global unemployment is expected to reach 207 million in 2022, a rise of 21 million on 2019 levels.[37]

Authoritarian Regimes – Shrinking Democratic Space

Trust in governments is declining, and authoritarianism is increasing. Less than 20 per cent of the world's population now live in what Freedom House defines as "a free country". Eritrea, North Korea, Somalia, Saudi Arabia, Belarus and China are among the countries with the lowest freedom score in the world.[38] The past 15 years have seen a growing democracy gap, with a consistent expansion of authoritarian rule and a decline in major democracies. Civic space, with respect for the right to assemble, organise and bargain, is under threat. In 2020, the level of democracy enjoyed by the average global citizen was down to levels last found around 1990, according to the V-Dem Institute. And although democratisation is still occurring around the world, it is predominantly taking place in small countries.[39]

Shrinking democratic space and increasing tyranny is a threat to human security, frequently resulting in the use of force and aggression. Non-democratic states not only threaten regional and global peace, but also fail to provide safety or security for their own citizens. The Institute for Economics and Peace found that both the fear of violence and the experience of violence were lower in full democracies than in flawed democracies, hybrid regimes and authoritarian regimes.[40]

Women often bear the brunt of democratic backsliding – facing increased opposition to gender equality and threats to previous progress on women's rights. The rights of women are particularly vulnerable in countries where the space for civil society is limited or shrinking.[41] Limited education and employment opportunities, restrictions on abortion rights, and a failure to address discrimination and gender-based violence all conspire to reduce the voice of women in decision-making and to reproduce male power structures.

Many people have not seen a dividend from democracy and feel left behind by society. This disconnect has led to a breakdown in trust between people and governments. With democracy on the back foot, corruption, populism and right wing extremism are filling the void in many countries. History teaches us that this situation leads to autocracy, aggression and competitive rivalry – rather than cooperation for collective progress. The rise of demagogues, in countries across the world, encourages divisions within and between peoples. Democracy can no longer be taken for granted, and citizens must understand their agency and power.[42]

Violations of democratic values go hand-in-hand with the repression of human rights. The annual Global Rights Index, from the International Trade Union Confederation, found that the number of countries where freedom of speech and assembly was denied or constrained increased from 56 in 2020 to 64 in 2021. There was also a rise in workers being detained and arrested around the world.[43]

Militarisation

At the time of the original commission, nuclear weapons were clearly the most powerful lethal force. Unfortunately, in the twenty-first century the threat of nuclear war remains undiminished. Scientists have now set the Doomsday Clock at 100 seconds to midnight for humanity. There are more than 13,000 nuclear warheads in the world today[44] – thousands of which are ready to be used in an instant and are far more powerful than those used on Hiroshima and Nagasaki.

Massive investments in faster, more lethal nuclear weapons, coupled with increasing tensions between nuclear-armed states, create a dangerous combination for conflict.

Meanwhile, discussion of the nuclear threat largely takes place away from the mainstream media and popular culture – with climate change replacing nuclear as the predominant existential danger in the public perception. Progress on disarmament has stalled in the past decades, and commitments to reduce weapons are disregarded. The Korean peninsula represents one area of particular concern, where nuclear tensions remain high and there is increasing militarisation. This is compounded by the fact that the Korean War never officially ended, with no peace treaty ever signed. Meanwhile, the deployment of conventional weapons continues to cause human misery all over the world. Battles between states and Islamist militants in Mali, Niger and Burkina Faso resulted in over 1,300 civilian fatalities in 2021.[45] Global instability and volatility, in Africa in particular, hinders economic and institutional development and creates an overarching feeling of insecurity within societies. The proliferation of small arms and light weapons initiate and exacerbate armed conflict and crime, as seen in Cabo Delgado in Mozambique, Ethiopia, Afghanistan, Haiti and Myanmar.

The economic and social burden of military spending was a central focus of the Palme Commission. 40 years later, military expenditure continues to rise and to divert funds from social and environmental investment. According to the Stockholm International Peace Research Institute (SIPRI), world military spending has been rising since the 1990s. In 2020 global military expenditure rose to almost $2 trillion, a 2.6% increase in real terms from 2019.[46]

Fuelled by corporate interests, the cost of global militarism stands in stark contrast to the shortage of money to tackle other challenges. This triggers a vicious circle – spending money on arms instead of people fosters inequality and stokes fear and division, which requires yet more military resources.

There is a clear gender dimension to weapons and arms control. As the UN Office of Disarmament Affairs says, "the ownership and use of arms is closely linked to specific expressions of masculinity related to control, power, domination and strength."[47] Men are predominantly the perpetrators of armed violence, and in 2018 men made up 92 per cent of the global deaths from firearms.[48] But small arms facilitate violence against women, frequently in the form of domestic and sexual violence. Additionally, women often bear the brunt of indirect impacts from armed violence, such as psychological trauma, impoverishment, exploitation and economic burdens.[49]

New technological developments – such as in the field of cyberspace, artificial intelligence, and drones – raise serious legal and moral questions. The use of computers or autonomous weapons systems to identify military targets presents a severe danger to international security. Algorithms cannot be relied on to decide on 'legitimate' military targets or follow international humanitarian law. The execution of human beings by algorithms, without human control, runs counter to the most basic tenets of international law and morality. In addition, the decision time with increasingly autonomous and digitalised systems is reduced, and a false alarm cannot be identified in time before the weapon hits.

Other new technological threats include cyber attacks on nuclear command, control and communications systems and the production of hypersonic missiles – with their manoeuvring capabilities, target ambiguity and the ability to reduce radar tracking. As a consequence, the concept of nuclear deterrence has become unreliable even for those who believed in it.

Forty years ago, the Palme Commission cautioned against the militarisation of outer space as a dangerous expansion of martial competition. This prediction appears prescient, with outer space becoming an increasingly contested and militarised environment. The deployment of weapons into outer space, whether offensive or defensive, is creating a new domain for conflict.

The Common Security 2022 recommendations are indications, or steps forward, in the process of removing the threat of nuclear annihilation and turning around the 'supertanker' of war. They are practical steps, but also set out a vision for a better, safer world. They aim to motivate public opinion and have a positive impact on policy- and decision-makers about what is necessary and achievable.

Full report available at commonsecurity.org

Notes

1. See Annex 4 for the Palme Commission's Principles in full at commonsecurity.org
2. The White House (3 January 2022) Joint Statement of the Leaders of the Five Nuclear-Weapon States on Preventing Nuclear War and Avoiding Arms Races.
3. Ronald Reagan Presidential Library and Museums (21 November 1985) Joint Soviet-United States Statement on the Summit Meeting in Geneva.
4. UNDP (2022) *New threats to human security in the Anthropocene: Demanding greater solidarity.*
5. United Nations (2021) *Our Common Agenda – Report of the Secretary-General.*
6. UN (1945) United Nations Charter. Preamble.
7. UN (1945) United Nations Charter. Article 2 (4).
8. United Nations Office of the High Commissioner for Human Rights (2011) *Guiding Principles on Business and Human Rights.*
9. Interview with Hilary Wainwright at the webinar *The World After Covid-19: Invest in Peace and Development not in War and Conflict* (15 February 2022).
10. ICAN (2020) *Enough Is Enough: 2019 Global Nuclear Weapons Spending.*
11. China, France, Germany, Iran, Russia, United Kingdom, United States of America (withdrawn), European Union
12. Interview with Hans Dahlgren at the Common Security 2022 Launch (14 June 2021).
13. Independent Commission on Disarmament and Security Issues (1982) *Common Security: A Programme for Disarmament* (London: Pan World Affairs). Page ix.
14. Independent Commission on Disarmament and Security Issues (1982) *Common Security: A Programme for Disarmament* (London: Pan World Affairs). Page 140-181.
15. Interview with Hans Dahlgren at the Common Security 2022 Launch (14 June 2021).
16. Heidelberg Institute for International Conflict Research (2021) *Conflict Barometer.*
17. United Nations (10 January 2021) Secretary-General's Remarks at the Commemoration of the 75th Anniversary of the First Meeting of the United Nations General Assembly [as delivered].
18. Interview with Michael Brozska from SIPRI at the webinar *The World After Covid-19: Invest in Peace and Development not in War and Conflict* (15 February 2022).
19. UN Women (2015) A Global Study on the Implementation of United Nations Security Council Resolution 1325.
20. Council on Foreign Relations (2020) *Women's Participation in Peace Processes.*
21. UN (Jan 2022) Peacebuilding and sustaining peace: Report of the Secretary-General A/76/668–S/2022/66. Para. 3, page 2.
22. PowerPoint by Ulrich Eberle (Fellow, Future of Conflict, International Crisis Group) during the webinar *There is Need for a Common Agenda for Peace and Climate* (19th October 2021).
23. The Intergovernmental Panel on Climate Change (IPCC) (2022) *Climate Change 2022: Impacts, Adaptation and Vulnerability.*
24. Georgetown Institute for Women, Peace and Security (2021) *The Climate-Gender-Conflict Nexus: Amplifying women's contributions at the grassroots.*
25. Institute for Economics and Peace (2021) *Ecological Threat Report 2021: Understanding Ecological Threats, Resilience and Peace.*
26. International Labour Organization (1919) Preamble to the ILO Constitution.
27. Independent Commission on Disarmament and Security Issues (1982) *Common Security: A Programme for Disarmament* (London: Pan World Affairs). Page 130.

28. Institute for Economics and Peace (2022) *Global Terrorism Index 2022: Measuring the Impact of Terrorism*. Page 5.
29. Oxfam International website.
30. Report of the Special Rapporteur on Extreme Poverty and Human Rights, Olivier De Schutter (July 2021) *The Persistence of Poverty: how real equality can break the vicious cycles*. Page 13.
31. Georgetown Institute for Women, Peace and Security (2021) *The Climate-Gender-Conflict Nexus: Amplifying women's contributions at the grassroots*.
32. UNICEF (2021) UNICEF Primary Education Data.
33. World Bank (2020) *Poverty and Shared Prosperity 2020: Reversals of Fortune*.
34. Oxfam International (2022) *Inequality Kills: The unparalleled action needed to combat unprecedented inequality in the wake of COVID-19*.
35. Institute for Economics and Peace (2021) *Global Peace Index 2021: Measuring Peace in a Complex World*.
36. International Labour Organization (2022) *World Employment and Social Outlook: Trends 2022*. Page 13.
37. International Labour Organization (2022) *World Employment and Social Outlook: Trends 2022*.
38. Freedom House (2021) *Freedom in the World 2021: Democracy Under Siege*.
39. V-Dem Institute (2021) Autocratization Turns Viral: Democracy Report 2021.
40. Institute for Economics and Peace (2021) *Global Peace Index 2021: Measuring Peace in a Complex World*. Page 54.
41. UN Women (2020) *Democratic backsliding and the backlash against women's rights: Understanding the current challenges for feminist politics*.
42. Barbara F. Walter (2022) *How Civil Wars Start - And How to Stop Them* (London: Viking).
43. International Trade Union Confederation (2021) *Global Rights Index*.
44. Stockholm International Peace Research Institute (2021) *SIPRI Yearbook 2021: Armaments, Disarmament and International Security*. Page 17.
45. International Crisis Group. *Ten Conflicts to Watch in 2022*.
46. Stockholm International Peace Research Institute (2021) SIPRI Military Expenditure Database.
47. UNODA (2018) *Securing Our Common Future: An Agenda for Disarmament*. Page 39.
48. Small Arms Survey (2018) *Global Violent Deaths Database*.
49. UNODA (2018) *Securing Our Common Future: An Agenda for Disarmament*. Page 39.

Nuclear-weapon-free zones

Ending the balance of terror

The Independent Commission on Disarmament and Security Isssues

First published in 1985, these selections from Common Security: A Blueprint for Survival *illustrate the important role played by the concepts and practice of developing nuclear-weapon-free zones in ending what Olof Palme described as the nuclear 'balance of terror'.*

From Olof Palme's introduction to Common Security: A Blueprint for Survival

Our report expresses our deep concern at the worsening international situation, and at the drift towards war that so many perceive today. We are totally agreed that there is no such thing as a nuclear war that can be won. An all-out nuclear war would mean unprecedented destruction, maybe the extinction of the human species. A so-called limited nuclear war would almost inevitably develop into total nuclear conflagration ...

On the basis of this strategy of common security, we discussed practical proposals to achieve arms limitation and disarmament. The long-term goal in the promotion of peace must be general and complete disarmament. But the Commission sees its task as being to consider a gradual process in that direction, to curb and reverse the arms race. We do not propose unilateral action by any country. We clearly see the need for balanced and negotiated reduction in arms.

Our aim has been to promote a downward spiral in armaments. We have elaborated a broad programme for reducing the nuclear threat, including major reductions in all types of strategic nuclear system[s]. We propose the establishment of a battlefield-nuclear-weapon-free zone starting in Central Europe. We also propose a chemical-weapon-free zone in Europe. Even the process of beginning to negotiate such limitations, we consider, would reduce political tension in Europe ...

We also emphasize the importance of regional approaches to security. We propose to strengthen regional security by creating zones of peace, nuclear-weapon-free zones, and by establishing regional conferences on security and cooperation similar to the one set up in Helsinki for Europe. We believe that regional discussions – including negotiations leading to chemical-weapon and battlefield-nuclear-weapon-free zones in Europe – can play an important role in achieving common security in all parts of the world.

* * * *

Reducing the nuclear threat in Europe

The nuclear arsenals in Europe are awesome. Furthermore, the Commission is deeply concerned about those nuclear postures and doctrines which dangerously and erroneously suggest that it may be possible to fight and 'win' a limited nuclear war. In the event of a crisis their effect could be to drive the contending forces across the threshold of a nuclear war. The Commission is convinced that there must be substantial reductions in the nuclear stockpile leading to denuclearisation in Europe and eventually to a world free of nuclear weapons. A necessary precondition is a negotiated agreement on substantial mutual force reductions establishing and guaranteeing an approximate parity of conventional forces between the two major alliances.

Therefore, the Commission supports a negotiated agreement for approximate parity in conventional forces between the two alliances. Such an agreement would facilitate reductions in nuclear weapons and a reordering of the priority now accorded to nuclear arms in military contingency planning.

The Commission has devoted much time and effort to examining various alternative ways for brining these changes about. Among the alternatives studied was nuclear-weapon-free zones, which are dealt with in Section 5.3 concerning regional security arrangements. It should be remembered in this connection that some countries in Europe do not belong to any of the military alliances and have renounced the acquisition of nuclear arms.

Here we propose a functional approach concentrating on specific weapons and classes of weapon. *Our proposal for the gradual removal of the nuclear threat posed to Europe includes establishment of a battlefield-nuclear-weapon-free zone and measures to strengthen the nuclear threshold and reduce pressure for the early use of nuclear weapons, and substantial reductions in all categories of intermediate-(medium-) and shorter-range nuclear weapons which threaten Europe.*

(a) A battlefield-nuclear-weapon-free zone in Europe. We call special attention to the dangers posed by those nuclear weapons whose delivery systems are deployed in considerable numbers to forward positions in Europe. These are known as 'battlefield' nuclear weapons. A large portion of NATO's and the Warsaw Pact's nuclear munitions in Europe are of this type. The weapons are designed and deployed to provide support to ground forces in direct contact with forces of the opponent. Their delivery systems have ranges up to 150 kilometres, and are primarily short-range rockets, mines, and artillery. Most of the delivery systems are dual-capable, i.e. they can fire either conventional munitions or nuclear munitions.

Because of their deployment in forward areas battlefield nuclear weapons run the risk of being overrun early in an armed conflict. Maintaining command and control over such weapons in 'the fog of war' would be difficult. Pressures for delegation of authority to use nuclear weapons to local commanders and for their early use would be strong. The danger of crossing the nuclear threshold and of further escalation could become acute. It should be remembered in this connection that the areas close to the East-West border in Central Europe are densely populated and contain large industrial concentrations.

The Commission recommends the establishment of a battle-field-nuclear-weapon-free zone, starting with Central Europe and extending ultimately from the northern to the southern flanks of the two alliances. This scheme would be implemented in the context of an agreement on parity and mutual force reductions in Central Europe. No nuclear munitions would be permitted in the zone.

Storage sites for nuclear munitions also would be prohibited. Manoeuvres simulating nuclear operations would not be allowed in the zone. Preparations for the emplacement of atomic demolition munitions and storage of such weapons would be prohibited.

There also would be rules governing the presence in the zone of artillery and short-range missiles that could be adapted for both nuclear and conventional use. The geographic definition of the zone should be determined through negotiations, taking into account the relevant circumstances in the areas involved, but for illustrative purposes, a width of 150 kilometres on both sides may be suggested. Provisions for verifying compliance with these prohibitions would be negotiated. They would have to include a limited number of on-site inspections in the zone on a challenge basis.

The Commission recognizes that nuclear munitions may be brought back to the forward areas in wartime, and that nuclear weapons may be delivered by aircraft and other longer range systems. However, we consider the establishment of the proposed zone an important confidence-building measure which would raise the nuclear threshold and reduce some of the pressures for early use of nuclear weapons. It is consistent with our rejection of limited nuclear war as a matter of deliberate policy.

The agreement for withdrawal of 'battlefield' nuclear weapons from the forward zone should be followed by substantial reductions in the number of nuclear munitions in Europe with adequate measures of verification.

* * * *

Nuclear-weapon-free zones

The Commission believes that the establishment of nuclear-weapons-free zones on the basis of arrangements freely arrived at among the states of the region or sub-region concerned, constitutes an important step towards non-proliferation, common security and disarmament. They could provide mutual reassurance to states preferring not to acquire or allow deployment of nuclear weapons as long as neighbouring states exercise similar restraint. This would improve the chances for the region not to become enveloped in the competition of the nuclear-weapon states. The nuclear-weapon states would have to undertake a binding commitment to respect the status of the zone, and not to use or threaten to use nuclear weapons against the states of the zone.

The Treaty of Tlatelolco, prohibiting nuclear weapons in Latin America, is a path-breaking regional agreement in this field. A party to it is not bound, though, until all the signatories have completed ratification, unless it waives this condition. Brazil and Chile have not done so. At present the treaty is in force for twenty-two Latin American states. Argentina has signed but not ratified the treaty. Cuba has neither signed nor ratified. The Commission strongly urges all states concerned to adopt all relevant measures to ensure the full application of the treaty.

Proposals for creating a nuclear-weapons-free zone in Africa, the South Pacific, South Asia and the Middle East have been put forward in the United Nations and have received support in the General Assembly. The process of establishing nuclear-weapon-free zones in different parts of the world should be encouraged with the ultimate objective of achieving a world entirely free of nuclear weapons.

Should it prove impossible to agree on legally defined nuclear-weapon-free zones, states could, as an interim measure, pledge themselves not to become the first to introduce nuclear weapons in the region. The nuclear-weapons states would have to guarantee the countries concerned that they would not be threatened or attacked with such weapons.

Nuclear-Weapon-Free Zones
How they work

Tom Unterrainer

Global Tinderbox

Excerpt from 'Global Tinderbox: Time for Europe's Nuclear-Weapon-Free Zone' published in The Spokesman 141 (2019).

If the Intermediate Nuclear Forces Treaty arose, at least in part, from the campaign for a nuclear weapon-free zone in Europe, then it acted as an important instrument against the threat that Europe could become an actual 'theatre' of nuclear war. Such a function is an essential component of NWFZ proposals. It has been suggested that the INF Treaty, in combination with the START 1 Treaty and 'Presidential Nuclear Initiatives' signed in 1991 and the 1992 Lisbon Protocol, combined – to all intents and purposes – to create a NWFZ in the Baltic States, Belarus, Bulgaria, the Czech Republic, Hungary, Moldova, Poland, Romania, Slovakia, and Ukraine.[1] This combination of states composed the 'core group' of a NWFZ proposed by Belarus in 1990.[2] The states in the core group have no nuclear weapons deployed within their boundaries. With the unilateral withdrawal of the US from the INF Treaty, this arrangement is under severe threat.

Threats to this arrangement are of some considerable consequence, not only due to the likely disestablishment of a quasi-NWFZ in and of itself but because NWFZ's carry the function of reducing risks of proliferation and escalation. The location of a quasi-NWFZ in the geographical periphery of Russia is of obvious importance and functionality:

"To the extent that the incentive to acquire nuclear weapons may emerge from regional considerations, the establishment of areas free of nuclear weapons is an important asset for the cause of nuclear nonproliferation. Countries confident that their enemies in the region do not possess nuclear weapons may not be inclined to acquire such weapons themselves."[3]

More broadly, the objectives of NWFZs were deliberated in some detail in a 1976 report by the United Nations Committee on Disarmament:

"the purpose of nuclear-weapon-free zones is to provide additional means for averting nuclear-weapon proliferation and halting the nuclear-arms race ... It is thus argued that [NWFZs] provide complementary machinery to other collateral measures of disarmament, non-proliferation of nuclear weapons and the development of peaceful uses of nuclear energy. Most experts felt that [NWFZs] must not be regarded as alternatives to the principle of the Treaty on the Non-Proliferation of Nuclear Weapons ... but should be entirely consistent with the objectives of the Treaty."[4]

The complementary nature of NWFZ proposals is important to emphasise. Any proposal for a new initiative for the creation of a European NWFZ should be seen as a specific measure in response to the proposed US withdrawal from the INF Treaty and not as an alternative to existing disarmament measures such as the Treaty on the Prohibition of Nuclear Weapons.[5] In fact, encouraging the creation of NWFZs is the responsibility of signatories to the Treaty on Non-Proliferation of Nuclear Weapons (NPT). In the action plan agreed at the 2010 NPT Review Conference, Action 9 states:

"**Action 9**: The establishment of further nuclear-weapon-free zones, where appropriate, on the basis of arrangements freely arrived at among States of the region concerned, and in accordance with the 1999 Guidelines of the United Nations Disarmament Commission, is encouraged. All concerned States are encouraged to ratify the nuclear-weapon-free zone treaties and their relevant protocols, and to constructively consult and cooperate to bring about the entry into force of the relevant legally binding protocols of all such nuclear-weapon free zones treaties, which include negative security assurances. The concerned States are encouraged to review any related reservations."[6]

So the basis for the creation of a NWFZ in Europe is established, but what – beyond a response to the destruction of the INF – could be its main objectives? The 2016 Peace Research Institute Frankfurt (PRIF) working paper, *A Nuclear Weapon-Free-Zone in Europe: Concepts-Problems-Chances*,[7] outlines a number of such objectives: 1. Security objectives in the narrow sense, 2. Political-symbolic objectives and 3. Adapting defence policies to the political situation in Europe. More detail is given within each of the three objectives, as outlined below:

1. Security objectives in the narrow sense

Confidence-building in the regional neighbourhood: "All states in the region are loyal parties to the NPT, and for many of them, membership goes beyond compliance and involves active promotion of the spirit and letter of that treaty."[8] Acting upon Action Point 9 of the 2010 NPT Review Conference would build and reinforce trust amongst regional signatories to the NPT, and would signal to neighbours – Russia in particular – that no threat is posed.

Irreversibility and Stability: The creation of the NWFZ in Europe would be the result of a legally binding, verifiable and therefore "hard to revoke"[9] arrangement.

Immunizing the region against the consequences of a nuclear confrontation: "one objective of any NWFZ has always been to protect the region concerned against becoming a nuclear battleground".[10]

2. Political-symbolic objectives

Strengthening the non-proliferation regime: Developing a NWFZ in Europe would mean signatories to the NPT acting on the 2010 Review Conference Action Plan. Such an act could only reinforce existing arms control and disarmament regimes.

Fostering nuclear disarmament: "Sub-strategic nuclear weapons are today one of the most nagging issues for nuclear disarmament ... A NWFZ in Europe would intend to, eventually, cover an area in which NATO's sub-strategic nuclear weapons are presently sited and to stimulate adequate reciprocal concessions by Russia concerning her capabilities in the same weapons category".[11]

Helping delegitimize nuclear weapons/provoking debate: As the PRIF study points out, the legitimacy of nuclear weapons as an issue of debate has never been "dormant". There have, however, been identifiable periods when debate and discussion adopted a much higher pitch than usual. Destruction of the INF should be an opportunity for the debate to gain traction and the proposal for a NWFZ in Europe can only boost such debates.

3. Adapting defence policies to the political situation in Europe

"One of the most frequently heard observations by non-Europeans is the disconnect between the nuclear constellation and the political situation in Europe. The relation between the West and Russia is not without disputes and occasional tensions ... but the idea of a war against each other sounds still far-fetched."[12]

Developments since the PRIF study was published now make it much easier to imagine war, even nuclear war, breaking out between "the West and Russia". Further, the general political situation in Europe has deteriorated markedly in the three years since the PRIF study, much 'adaptation' of defence policies is already underway.[13] The development of plans for the NWFZ in Europe would add something definitively more positive to the current debate and could unleash an all-too-necessary political counter-dynamic to the current direction of travel.

An important aspect of any proposal for a NWFZ in Europe is that it would, in fact, benefit from being part of an international system of such zones. In his indispensable study, *Security without Nuclear Deterrence*, Commander Robert Green notes:

"Every year since 1996 the UN General Assembly has adopted a resolution introduced by Brazil calling upon the states parties and signatories to the regional NWFZ treaties 'to promote the nuclear weapon free status of the Southern Hemisphere and adjacent areas', and to explore and promote further cooperation among themselves."[14]

The first conference of states already participating in NWFZs took place in Mexico in April 2005. The declaration adopted by the conference reaffirmed a commitment to the "consolidation, strengthening and expansion of NWFZs, the prevention of nuclear proliferation and the achievement of a nuclear weapons free world."[15] So not only do signatories to the NPT share a commitment to establish NWFZs, but existing such zones are committed to their expansion.

This leaves the rather important question of 'who', or 'what', will have the capacity to drive forward the call for the NWFZ in Europe.

Notes

1. Finaud, Mark (2014) *The Experience of Nuclear Weapon-Free Zones*, BASIC. Source: http://www.basicint.org/publications/marc-finaud/2014/experience-nuclear-weapon-free-zones

2. Non-core states included Albania, Austria, Finland, Sweden and the states of the former Yugoslavia, with Norway, Denmark and Germany proposed as additional members. Source: hwww.basicint.org/publications/marc-finaud/2014/ experience-nuclear-weapon-free-zones. See also fas.org/programs/ssp/nukes/ ArmsControl_NEW/nonproliferation/NFZ/NP-NFZ-CF.html for more on the Belarus proposals of 1990.

3. Goldblat, Joseph (1997) 'Nuclear-Weapon-Free Zones: A History and Assessment', *The Nonproliferation Review*, Spring-Summer 1997

4. *Comprehensive Study of the Question of Nuclear-Weapon-Free Zones in all its Aspects*, Special Report of the Conference of the Committee on Disarmament, United Nations, New York, 1976

5. See www.icanw.org/why-a-ban/positions/ for the most recent information on the status of the TPNW

6. Text accessed at https://dfat.gov.au/international-relations/security/non-proliferation-disarmament-arms-control/policies-agreements-treaties/treaty-on-the-non-proliferation-of-nuclear-weapons/Pages/2010-npt-review-conference-64-point-action-plan.aspx

7. Müller, Harald et al (2016) *A Nuclear Weapon-Free Zone in Europe: Concepts-Problems-Chances*, PRIF Working Paper No. 27, January 2016

8. Ibid

9. Ibid

10. Ibid

11. Ibid

12. Ibid

13. See Lösing, Sabine (2018) 'Militarising Europe Again', *Europe for the Many*, The Spokesman, issue 140, Spokesman, Nottingham

14. Green, Robert (2018) *Security without Nuclear Deterrence*, Spokesman, Nottingham

15. Ibid

A Soviet View

A. N. Kalyadin

Alexander Kalyadin was a prolific Soviet scholar and writer on international relations. Problems of Common Security *compiled papers by the Scientific Research Council on Peace and Disarmament and the Soviet Peace Fund. It was edited by V. S. Shaposhnikov and published in the USSR in 1984.*

Published two years after the Palme Commission report, Problems of Common Security *is a comprehensive exposition of Soviet thinking at the time. This publication of an edited version of Alexander Kalyadin's essay on 'Nuclear-Free Zones' is not an endorsement of the work in which it is contained, but a demonstration of the seriousness with which the concept of such zones was taken in the USSR and a contribution to recovering and explaining them.*

The Concept of a Nuclear-Free Zone

Washington's massive arms build-up, the Pentagon's plans of "limited" and "protracted" nuclear wars in various regions of the globe, the establishment of US nuclear bases on foreign territories, and the attempts to involve numerous countries in US military plans have lately given a new impetus to the idea of creating nuclear-free zones [i.e. geographic zones where nuclear weapons are to be neither developed, nor deployed]. Its advocates believe that the further strengthening of their countries' nuclear-free status would guarantee their non-involvement in a nuclear conflict. This idea enjoys broad popularity, which is evidenced by the relevant proposals from a number of governments, its support by the UN and other international organisations, and the mass anti-nuclear demonstrations, whose participants increasingly call for creating nuclear-weapon-free zones. The viability of this idea has also been confirmed by practical experience in securing a nuclear-free status for the Latin American countries, a status that was formalised by the 1967 Treaty for the Prohibition of Nuclear Weapons in Latin America (Treaty of Tlatelolco).

The issue of nuclear-free zones has been a subject of discussion by the United Nations for a number of years. UN General Assembly resolutions and other UN documents have formulated and agreed upon concrete provisions making up the concept 'nuclear-weapon-free zone', or 'nuclear-free zone'.

These documents have, above all, formulated some general principles of the concept, consisting essentially in that states included in such zones shall promise neither to purchase and develop nuclear weapons, nor to admit foreign nuclear weapons into those zones, while states that already possess nuclear weapons shall in turn promise to strictly respect the nuclear-weapon-free zone status and refrain from using or threatening to use nuclear weapons against states situated in such zones. The UN General Assembly resolutions favouring the creation of nuclear-weapon-free zones in various regions of the globe and adopted in recent years with the backing of an overwhelming majority of UN members helped to make this idea become more popular.

Significantly, today's massive anti-war movement throughout the world is showing growing interest in the idea of nuclear-free zones. Calls for the creation of such zones have become an essential element in the slogans of mass anti-war demonstrations. In some countries there are movements for creating nuclear-free zones both on a national and local scale. It is not by chance that this movement has become especially widespread in Western Europe. It was, in effect, a response to the NATO leaders' decision to deploy new medium-range US nuclear missiles in several West European states and to the readiness of US strategists to use the territories of their West European NATO allies as a theatre of war involving the use of nuclear weapons. The abrupt upsurge in the anti-nuclear movement in Western Europe was chiefly motivated by the West European peoples' increased awareness of the danger of these actions. The participants in the movement demand more resolutely than before that their governments alienate themselves from the dangerous nuclear plans of the United States and NATO, remove nuclear weapons from their territories and proclaim them nuclear-free zones. In some countries, the movement for nuclear-free zones has spread to municipal bodies.

As a result of a powerful anti-nuclear movement, many towns, settlements and other administrative centres in Britain, The Netherlands, Belgium and West Germany were declared nuclear-free zones, where local authorities prohibit the deployment, transportation and production of nuclear weapons. And though their national governments have declared they would ignore such resolutions, their moral and political significance is great for they symbolise the rejection by the broad masses of population of nuclear weapons, the nuclear arms race, and the strategy of nuclear intimidation, and show the desire of those masses to make a concrete contribution to the struggle for eliminating the threat of nuclear war and for curbing the nuclear arms race ...

[I]t was the Soviet Union which tabled, on 27 March 1956, a proposal at the UN Disarmament Commission to create a zone of limitation and inspection of armaments in Europe ... The proposal suggested that an agreement be reached to ban the deployment of nuclear-armed units and all other types of atomic and hydrogen weapons in a zone that would include the territories of the German Democratic Republic and the Federal Republic of Germany, and also their neighbouring states. In fact, this proposal contained the contours of future plans for creating nuclear-free zones. It was further elaborated in Poland's proposal (1957) [The Rapacki Plan] to create a nuclear-free zone in Central Europe. Under the Polish plan, the participants (Poland, Czechoslovakia, the GDR, and the FRG) were to have undertaken not to produce, purchase or deploy nuclear weapons on their territories. The nuclear powers were to have promised not to hand over nuclear weapons to the participants, not to deploy them there, or use them against the territory of the said nuclear-free zone. The Polish plan also provided for measures to control the implementation of such an agreement. The USSR declared its support for the Polish proposal and expressed readiness to adhere to its commitments. A similar statement was made by Czechoslovakia and the GDR.

It is not accidental that the idea of creating a nuclear-free zone was initially suggested in regard to Central Europe, a region where the need to prevent nuclear confrontation had become especially urgent already at that time. However, the United States and its NATO allies took a negative stand towards this issue, showing no desire to undertake any commitments not to deploy or use nuclear weapons in Central Europe.

In subsequent years, the idea of creating nuclear-free zones to strengthen regional security was backed by many countries. It was amplified in various projects for establishing nuclear-free zones in respective continents, regions and countries. These projects reflected the specific features of the military-political situation in individual regions, the stands of individual governments and the public, and changes in the world situation as a whole.

In determining its attitude to the establishment of nuclear-free zones in specific regions, the USSR proceeds from the assumption that the main task of any nuclear-free zone is to prevent the proliferation of nuclear weapons on a regional scale, and to protect the states of the region in question from becoming involved in a nuclear conflict.

In assessing concrete projects, the question that naturally arises is what should be the prerequisites for creating an effective, totally nuclear-free zone. There can, of course, be no single model. Every region has its own specifics, which should be taken into account in drafting a relevant agreement. However, this does not exclude the need for working out certain general criteria for a nuclear-free zone, ensuing from the tasks facing such zones and from their role within the system of international security.

These criteria stem primarily from the principal tasks any nuclear-free zone is called upon to resolve. They include a pledge by the participating states not to produce and purchase nuclear weapons or other nuclear explosive devices, not to exercise direct or indirect control over such arms, and also not to allow the presence of foreign nuclear weapons in the zone. It is also important for such a zone to be really free of nuclear arms: the relevant agreement must not have any loopholes that would make it possible to violate the zone's nuclear-free status. On their part, the nuclear states would have to strictly respect the zone's nuclear-free status and not use or threaten to use nuclear weapons against its participants. An agreement on a nuclear-free zone would have to conform with the existing norms of international law. An important factor in making a nuclear-free zone effective would be the establishment of a reliable mechanism to control the fulfilment of commitments undertaken by the nations participating in such a zone. Being a regional measure, a nuclear-free zone must have its distinctive features as compared with global measures. However, inasmuch as it is assumed that the nuclear states would have to undertake definite commitments in regard to the states participating in a nuclear-free zone, the need for the former to take part in relevant talks is obvious ...

As for the geographical limits of nuclear-free zones, as is apparent from the proposals put up by various governments, such zones may include entire continents, geographical regions, groups of countries, and individual states. In any case, such limits must be distinctly specified by consent of all the parties concerned ...

Regional Projects for Nuclear-Free Zones

In Europe, the movement for establishing nuclear-free zones is mounting, and concrete actions are being taken in this direction by various governments. This is seen, among other things, in a number of European states' initiative to officially formalise their nuclear-free status, strengthen the regime of nuclear non-proliferation, and consolidate regional stability.

Northern Europe is a region where such possibilities are rated highly. Unlike Western Europe now living literally on a nuclear volcano, Northern Europe is still free of nuclear weapons. The countries of Northern Europe have achieved a relatively high level of good-neighbour relations, albeit Norway and Denmark are NATO members, and Finland and Sweden are not. The four are signatories to the Non-Proliferation Treaty. They are aware of the dangerous consequences of the new US and NATO nuclear missile plans in Europe, especially those that may result from the recent deployment of US medium-range nuclear missiles in Western Europe. This increases the danger of their involvement in a nuclear conflict and makes the task of establishing a nuclear-free zone in Northern Europe especially urgent ...

As a result, social and political circles in Norway and Denmark are showing an increasing tendency towards formalising the nuclear-free status of the Scandinavian region within the framework of an international agreement so as to protect the region from the danger of being involved in a nuclear conflict and in NATO's nuclear strategy.

Finland came out in active support of the idea of establishing a nuclear-weapon-free zone in Northern Europe. On 28 May 1963, the Finnish President proposed that the Scandinavian countries create such a zone and confirm by means of mutual commitments the absence of nuclear weapons in the area without damaging the security of those countries or violating the balance of forces in the world. In May 1978, the President developed this concept by proposing to work out a Scandinavian arms control agreement which would be chiefly aimed at protecting the Scandinavian countries from the potential consequences of a nuclear strategy, in general, and from new nuclear technology, in particular. The Finnish government made proposals to begin appropriate talks between the Scandinavian states with the participation of nuclear states in the talks. This has launched a discussion among socio-political circles in the Scandinavian countries, in the course of which various aspects of the question of establishing such a zone were examined. The discussion has noticeably concretised the idea of establishing a nuclear-free zone in Northern Europe ...

In 1982, over 2.5 million Danes, Finns, Norwegians and Swedes put their signatures under the Appeal for a Nuclear-Free North. And despite the increased activity of forces seeking to prevent the implementation of this plan, it meets with response and support among people who side with different political parties and mass public organisations, and also among government circles in the Scandinavian countries. The struggle for consolidating the nuclear-free status of Northern Europe remains a major trend in the political life of the countries of the region.

The *Balkans* is also a region where more favourable prospects have recently come to light for establishing a nuclear-free zone. The political climate has significantly improved there, and in the present-day tense international situation life in the Balkans is relatively quiet. The Balkan countries show a strong desire not only for the results of detente to be preserved, but also multiplied to give a positive political impetus to Europe ...

Following the victory of the democratic forces at the October 1981 parliamentary elections in Greece, the new cabinet formed by the Panhellenic Socialist Movement (PASOK) declared the Greek intention to turn the Balkans into a nuclear-free zone and to reject the deployment of nuclear arms on Greek territory. This has opened up new prospects for establishing that zone. When Greek Prime Minister Andreas Papandreo visited Sofia in 1982, it was noted that the initiative to turn the Balkans into a nuclear-free zone met the interests of the Balkan peoples and helped to improve the international climate and to gradually turn Europe into a continent free of nuclear weapons. Concrete steps have been made in this direction. In 1982, Bulgaria proposed holding a Balkan summit meeting to discuss the proposal for turning the Balkans into a nuclear-free zone. The Bulgarian initiative met positive responses in Yugoslavia, Romania, and Greece. It should be remembered, however, that today the Balkan Peninsula is where the line of direct contact between the Warsaw Treaty and NATO countries passes and where external imperialist forces, seeking to destabilise the situation and preserve the foreign military bases, are active. These factors complicate the task of establishing a nuclear-free zone there, but at the same time they make this task especially urgent and politically significant ...

The Mediterranean. In 1963, the USSR suggested a project for turning the entire Mediterranean area into a nuclear-missile-free zone. The Soviet government declared its readiness to pledge not to deploy nuclear weapons and their delivery vehicles in the Mediterranean implying that similar pledges would be made by other states, too. The USSR also proposed that, after that region has been declared a nuclear-free zone, the USSR and the United States should give joint "reliable guarantees that in the event of any military complication, the Mediterranean Sea area would be regarded as being outside the sphere of nuclear weapons." Subsequently, the USSR supplemented this proposal with new ideas, such as reaching international agreements on:

– extending to the Mediterranean the confidence-building measures in military matters that have already proved effective in international practice;
– co-ordinating the reduction of armed forces in the area;
– withdrawing nuclear weapons carriers from the Mediterranean;
– refusing to deploy nuclear weapons on the territories of non-nuclear Mediterranean countries;
– undertaking that the nuclear states refrain from using nuclear weapons against any Mediterranean country that does not allow other nations to deploy such weapons on its territory ...

Earlier, we have spoken of the 25-year-old plan of the socialist countries to establish a nuclear-free zone in *Central Europe.* The plan was rejected by the United States which preferred to start building nuclear bases in West Germany and turning it into America's chief nuclear arsenal in Europe. This has resulted in the greater saturation of Central Europe with nuclear weaponry. The US nuclear arms build-up in the region following the well-known NATO missile decision of 12 December 1979 has aggravated the tense situation of nuclear confrontation in Central Europe. In this situation, the Swedish government proposed that the Warsaw Treaty countries and the NATO members establish in Europe a zone free of "theatre nuclear weapons", which would be approximately 300 km wide, i.e. extend for 150 km on both sides of their line of contact. Sweden proposed starting appropriate talks on the type of nuclear weapons deployed in Europe and in the seas around Europe. The USSR supported the Swedish proposal and spoke in favour of expanding the geographical limits of the zone free of theatre nuclear weapons so that those talks would really be an effective measure for reducing the nuclear threat.

Taking into consideration the main characteristics of the existing types of nuclear weapons (range, velocity, etc.), the increasing range of tactical missiles, and the capability of tactical aviation (one of the major components of the theatre nuclear weapons), the USSR suggested the establishment of a 500-600-km-wide zone, i.e. extending 250 to 300 km west and east of the line of contact of the Warsaw Treaty and NATO countries.

The USSR suggested that the establishment of this zone could be started in Central Europe within the framework of the Vienna talks on reducing armed forces and armaments in the region. The USSR declared readiness to take part in talks concerning the establishment of that zone, including its geographic dimensions and control measures ...

Yet, the Swedish proposal, which would have made it possible to significantly lower the level of military confrontation in Europe, had not become the subject of talks because of the negative attitudes of the United States and some NATO countries. They showed no interest in restricting tactical nuclear weapons, which would have had major significance for alleviating the tense situation of nuclear confrontation in Europe, for lessening the nuclear threat and for securing mutual trust among nations ...

[The] United States and the other Western nuclear powers have actually refused to commit themselves to pledges that would open the way to a real solution of the above-mentioned issues. Because of their negative stand, there is also no progress at the talks on strengthening security guarantees for the non nuclear states. The US and NATO ruling circles seek to have a choice of options for retaining their nuclear weapons on foreign territory, deploying them in places where they are still absent, and eventually using them.

This stand naturally reduces the possibility of finding generally acceptable solutions to establishing regional nuclear-free zones and formalising agreements concerning a nuclear-free status of specific countries. This also hampers the gradual lowering of the level of nuclear confrontation, both global and regional, and the elimination of the danger of a nuclear conflict.

94

The F Word

Mhairi Black has served as the Member of Parliament for Paisley and Renfrewshire since 2015. This is her speech to Parliament on 18 May 2022 in a debate on Economic Growth.

Mhairi Black MP

For a party that prides itself on the economy, the Tories have a shocking record of running it. Our economy has the slowest growth in the G7. We have greater regional inequality than almost any other developed nation. Food banks now do the job of Government in providing for families – families that are more often than not in work.

The Government could start solving this crisis by providing solutions, such as closing tax-avoidance loopholes or creating a windfall tax for energy companies. Instead, we get endless Bills paying lip service to a manufactured culture war. The priority is not the economy. It seems to be things like protecting freedom of speech, yet the Tories are the ones who banned schools in England from using sources that are not overtly pro-capitalist. They are cracking down on freedom of assembly and protest. They are privatising Channel 4, when the Culture Secretary did not even know that Channel 4 receives no public money, so the argument is not financial. When we consider, as the hon. Member for Rhondda (Chris Bryant) touched on earlier, that the Culture Secretary was once a key focus of a Channel 4 documentary about the influence that Christian fundamentalism has on UK politics, it becomes even more concerning that this decision is political and personal. It is not professional.

Most terrifying of all, however, is that the Government literally want to get rid of the Human Rights Act. That begs the question: for whom do they think rights have gone too far? Do they know how scary it is to sit at home and wonder if it is you—is it your rights that are up for grabs? We have witnessed Windrush. Our economic strategy is to open our doors to the rest of the world when we need their hard work and then chuck them out 50 years later without a word's notice. We tell our own citizens that their safety cannot be guaranteed in Rwanda, but we are perfectly happy to ship asylum seekers, people fleeing war and persecution, over to Rwanda as though they are cattle to be dealt with by someone else and despite knowing that the plan costs more than it will ever save.

This is just little England elites drunk on the memory of a British empire that no longer exists. We have the lowest pensions in Europe and the lowest sick pay. We pretend the minimum wage is a living wage when it is not. We miss our own economic targets time and again. We are happy to break international law. We are turning into a country where words hold no value.

Over the last 12 years, I fear we have been sleepwalking closer and closer to the F word. I know everyone is scared to say it for fear of sounding over the top or being accused of going too far, but I say this with all sincerity. When I say the F word, I am talking about fascism – fascism wrapped in red, white and blue. You may mock and you may disagree, but fascism does not come in with intentional evil plans or the introduction of leather jackboots. It does not happen like that. It happens subtly. It happens when we see Governments making decisions based on self-preservation, based on cronyism, based on anything that will keep them in power, when we see the concentration of power while avoiding any of the scrutiny or responsibility that comes with that power. It arrives under the guise of respectability and pride, which will then be refused to anyone who is deemed different. It arrives through the othering of people and the normalisation of human cruelty. I do not know how far down that road we are. Time will tell, but the things we do in the name of economic growth – the warning signs are there for everyone else to see, whether they admit it or not.

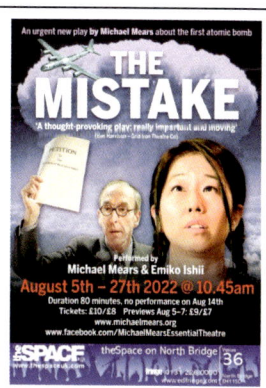

The Mistake by Michael Mears
1942. On a squash court in Chicago a dazzling experiment takes place, which three years later will destroy a city and change the world – forever. Through the lives of a brilliant Hungarian scientist, a daring American pilot and a devoted Japanese daughter, this powerful new play explores the events surrounding the catastrophic 'mistake' that launched our nuclear age.
www.michaelmears.org

Reviews

Memories

Sheila Rowbotham, *During to Hope: My Life in the 1970s*, Verso, 2021, hardback ISBN 9781839763892, £20

If you remember the 1970s ... I do and I was there, in Glasgow, Aberdeen and Nottingham and I remember parts with great clarity, parts only vaguely, and some parts I regret remembering at all. Sheila, on the other hand, has the utmost clarity as she kept a diary and journal throughout that tumultuous decade when she was a prominent activist in the women's liberation movement and leading historian.

Being prominent – as the writer of seminal texts published in the period – she knew 'everyone', so I found myself nodding at the names, Audrey Wise MP, historians Edward and Dorothy Thompson, Marsha Rowe from *Spare Rib*, May Hobbs of the Night Cleaners' Campaign, the libertarian Marxist doctor David Widgery among many; and the campaigns and organisations, the Institute for Workers' Control, the Claimants' Union, the campaign against Ted Heath's Industrial Relations Act, the various campaigns against those who would restrict abortion rights, to name just a few. On one of the latter I can remember an overnight minibus trip to London from Aberdeen to attend a demonstration, returning the next night. What it was to be young.

Of course, the 1970s did not spring from nowhere and the rise of the women's movement grew from small groups or networks: 'clusters of women's liberationists had also cohered in several towns and cities, and the Trotskyist-influenced *Socialist Woman* magazine based in Nottingham, had appeared'. Nottingham appears here and there in the text, not least as Paul Atkinson came from here, he being one of Sheila's long-term partners in the 'duogamy' she shared with David Widgery, both of whom had other partners. Not that Sheila was entirely into duogamy, at one time adding Bobby Campbell to the roster, Bea Campbell's former husband. What it was to be young ...

Sheila talks us through the rise and rise of the women's movement, and is honest about the crises it went through. These include its battles with 'Wages for Housework', the internal battles over hierarchy (some women thought that she should not have her name on her books as it created hierarchy), the move to recognise lesbians – which she approved of very much – and the later debates about whether, in short, men were the enemy.

This was not a position she held at any time, not least as she was teaching Workers' Educational Association (WEA) classes, which rooted her as well as giving her access to earlier generations of trade union activists (and in one case an elderly Jewish man who lived through the Russian Revolution). Astonishingly, men attended some of the early women's liberation conferences. The last time men attended saw the Maoist Harpal Brar drone on and on, refusing to leave the stage until he was dragged away by the University security. My women friends of that era talked over all these issues.

The 1970s was a period of industrial struggles: the great mining strikes of '72 and '74; Grunwick; the aforementioned Night Cleaners' Campaign among them. Night after night Rowbotham was out trying to unionise night cleaners. Ironically, over the last few years, the pop-up unions have had the success that eluded May Hobbs, Sheila and the big unions back then.

On the history front, Raphael Samuel's *History Workshop* was at its height and people went to great lengths to rediscover our political past, in Sheila's case this included Edward Carpenter and a 'pilgrimage' to Millthorpe in Derbyshire where he used to live and other sites associated with him. She remarks that she had to pinch herself on approaching Millthorpe to remember that Carpenter would not be there to meet her. I felt exactly the same on the first Edward Carpenter walk organised from Nottingham by the late Chris Richardson!

The national women's conferences fell away to be replaced by socialist feminist conferences, a description that fitted Sheila but caused her and others to struggle with the 'Leninist' model. She was still involved in campaigning but now, as a parent, this included organising with the Hackney Under-fives Campaign. At that time the word 'libertarian' had not yet been stolen by the right, and the left was in flux. The political group Big Flame was influential. There were debates on being 'in and against the state' — the important book of that title has recently been re-issued. But Sheila, Hilary Wainwright and Lynne Segal came together to publish – initially in a run of 100 copies – *Beyond the Fragments*, subtitled *Feminism and the Making of Socialism*. The 1970s ended with this title which is now in its third edition and, perhaps as much as anything, enabled Sheila to call her new book *Daring to Hope*.

This is an exciting read. I read it over a weekend. It's not just for oldsters who were there at the time. And there are moments of fun ... the chic Greek feminists who were not impressed with, shall we say, the downbeat style of living of the Hackney and Brixton Left, and the American feminists who were surprised at Sheila turning up for a lecture tour in the United States with a single dowdy dress (normally, of course, she wore dungarees). And there are moments of sadness – a long drive with Ruth First, talking non-stop on the last time they met: 'It was the last time I saw Ruth, who was about to leave Durham for a post as director of research at the Centre of African Studies in Mozambique. In 1982 she was assassinated by a parcel bomb ...' It was a salutary reminder that those days of hope were not welcomed by all.

Ross Bradshaw

Stalin the Bookworm

Geoffrey Roberts, *Stalin's Library: A Dictator and His Books*, Yale University Press, 2022, 272 pages, hardback ISBN 9780300179040, £25

Geoffrey Roberts is Emeritus Professor of History, University of Cork, and author of 11 other Stalin-related books. This one, lucid and jargon-free, comprises seven graphically-titled chapters, bookended by Introduction and Conclusion, buttressed by 70 pages of end notes often supplementing his text, Further Reading tips plus twenty formal titles, serviceable Index, thirteen black-white plates (no. 11 shows Stalin doodling marginalia on Alexei Tolstoy's 1942 play *Ivan Grozny* (*Ivan the Terrible*). Frequently here, as elsewhere, Stalin appends the word 'Teacher'. This has fortified the myth (expounded by Maureen Perry's *The Cult of Ivan the Terrible in Stalin's Russia*, 2000) that Ivan was Stalin's 'Teacher'. In fact, as Roberts shows, 'Teacher' was, unsurprisingly, Lenin (p. 62).

Roberts wastes no time denouncing Stalin as 'monster' and the like. He wants the complete man, downplaying 'moral revulsion'. As reported by Molotov, Stalin's dictum was 'if you want to know the people around you, find out what they read'. For Roberts, Stalin's annotations ('Pomenski') are 'the closest we shall ever get to the spontaneous Stalin' (p.4).

Roberts goes far beyond his title, providing a concise Soviet history from Stalin's birth to death and down to contemporary matters. This is familiar stuff, though useful for contexts, and will not be discussed here. My themes are his library and select passages where Roberts argues, usually convincingly, against other biographers, named or unspecified.

One pleasant surprise to many may be that Stalin wrote poetry in his youth. Five poems were published, a sixth suppressed. No reason why an evil person should not also try their hand at verse. Roman Emperor Nero is a prime example. Surviving fragments at least show a mastery of metrical smoothness. Having no Georgian, I rely on Roberts (p.40) for this translated extract from 'To The Moon':

Know well, those who once
Fell to the oppressor
Will rise again with hope
Above the holy mountain.

Remember that Stalin was often relying on translated texts as he knew only Georgian and Russian. Stalin's claim of fluency in German is doubted by Roberts. His efforts to learn English and French came to nothing. Putin, by contrast, is fluent in German, as Angela Merkel confirms, but shaky in English, though (surprisingly?) he knows basic Swedish. Like Stalin, he takes trouble to encourage his children to read. An online list of Putin's ten favourite authors includes Ernest Hemingway; his favourite Russian poet is Mikhail Lermontov.

Of the ancillary books recommended by Roberts, A. Kemp-Welch's *Stalin and the Literary Intelligentsia 1925-1939* is the most useful, and one should add Vitaly Shentalinsky's *The KGB's Literary Archive.*

There is one glaring oddity. Roberts makes the standard academic boast of a 'unique' approach. Now, Kindle users will find another item with the identical title, *Stalin's Library.* This is by Cambridge-based Svetlana Lokhova, a distinguished Sovietologist. It is actually a reproduction of her chapter ten in (ed.) Helen Fry's *Routledge International Handbook of Universities: Security and Intelligence Studies* (2019), providing a succinct description of Stalin's holdings, which some readers might prefer to Roberts' full-scale book. For all that I can see, Roberts never mentions this item, published three years before his own.

Nor does Roberts acknowledge (though he takes frequent pot-shots at him) the brief but lucid account in Simon Sebag Montefiore's superlative *Stalin: the Court of the Red Czar* (2004, pages 99-102), drawing heavily on Molotov as source, the latter crediting Stalin with a library of 20,000 volumes (other estimates range from 14 to 25,000 volumes). Molotov also commended Stalin's 'exceptional' knowledge of antiquity and mythology.

Roberts subjoins that Stalin's favourite marginal criticism was his 'mirthless' HA HA HA! — the ultimate term of abuse being 'Oh, Mama!' What would Freudians make of that?

Roberts provides examples of Stalin's commendations and criticisms.

The former include 'YES YES', 'GOOD', 'SPOT ON', 'AGREED'. The latter are often crude: 'NONSENSE', 'RUBBISH', 'FOOL', 'SCUMBAG'. Despite such vulgarities, the quality of some of Stalin's personal abuse is paralleled in the marginalia of classicist-poet A. E. Housman.

Lenin is predictably a major influence on Stalin's judgements. For easy instance, both detested Dostoevsky and the cult around him, dismissing him as a 'repulsive reactionary' and so on. Sometimes, we get a surprise. Stalin's fervent approval of agronomist Trofim Lysenko's false theories about crop rearing was notorious. Yet, one marginal comment on Lysenko is the lethal 'HA HA HA', embellished with a battery of sarcasms.

Such annotations have further value in that Stalin did not keep a diary or journal, much less did he contemplate an autobiography. He would put off would-be biographers, realizing they would simply churn out hagiographies, one of several indications that he did not hanker for a cult of personality. What he really wanted was official publication of his collected works. As the years passed, apart from his love of, and interference in, Russian films, he took on more and more editing, becoming Russia's leader in this field. Obviously, plenty of scope here for rewriting and 'updating' of history in Big Brother style, but Roberts does not go in for unremitting suspicions that he never did an honest job. Roberts also acquits Stalin of plagiarism in his own published works.

A supreme and ironic example is the case of Annabelle Bucar who, after working for the American Embassy in Moscow, defected to the Soviet Union and eventually wrote a 'tell-all' book about American diplomats. Stalin thought this would be an effective counter against American post-war 'spy mania'. A Russian publisher had asked Stalin's permission to issue a Russian translation. Stalin not only approved but edited the entire book himself. Talking of which, it's amusing to recall that in Tallin in 1999 there appeared a 'secret document' from the 1950s purportedly proving that Patriarch Alexy II was a KGB agent. American intelligence suspected it was ghost written by the Soviet Ministry of State Security.

Stalin was fascinated by American know-how in science and technology, and standards of living, its social injustices being exposed by his admiration for the works of Jack London. For a time, as did Orwell in the 1930s, Stalin looked to America as a likely standard-bearer of proletarian revolution. He attributed its failure to the weakness and corruption of American trade union leaders. Stalin had been deeply upset by the sudden death of Roosevelt. For his part, an impressionable Harry Truman proclaimed 'Stalin is Russia', a detail whose omission by other historians is deplored by Svetlana Lokhova. She also takes biographers to task for omitting Stalin's deep interest in intelligence gathering methods and techniques of code-breaking, special credit here going to the British.

Stalin acquired his first volume in 1925, not long after Lenin's death. A desire to emulate his 'Teacher' is obvious enough. It is also to be seen in the context of Bolshevik plans to make the masses literate book-lovers. To this end, a network of libraries was established, supervised by Krupskaya, Lenin's widow, who increasingly transformed editorship into censorship.

Stalin classified his books not by their authors but by their subject matter, leaving hand-written lists on how to sub-divide the manifold variations. Apart from Party documents, there were special sections reserved for Lenin (of course), Trotsky (no attempt here to airbrush him from history), Bukharin and fellow functionaries, Rosa Luxemburg and, naturally, his favourite, Maxim Gorky. As Lenin did, so Stalin organized and categorised favourite foreign classics (Shakespeare and company) — again, he relied on Russian translations. When he edited a 'secret' document known as the *Red Army Guide to the Battle for Moscow*, Stalin expunged all mentions of himself.

Even during his busiest moments, not excluding the war, Stalin claimed to read 500 pages a day, including 'mind-numbing' (Roberts) technical reports — something I would find hard to credit even in the case of Mrs Thatcher.

After Khrushchev's famous 'secret' denunciatory speech of Stalin in 1956, if not before, Stalin's library was broken up. Some 14,000 volumes were dispersed among various libraries, leaving a residue of approximately 5,000, including 400 with annotations in blue or red pencil.

Taken together, Roberts and Lokhova provide an invaluable guide to these most fascinating documents. As said, Roberts, in addition to his considerable other merits, is courteous but sharp in his criticisms of other biographers for various sins of commission and omission. For example, he shows at length that Stalin did *not* poison his second wife, Nadia, and probably did *not* organize the assassination of Kirov.

Pending discovery of new materials, Roberts (again, not forgetting Lokhova) can — unlike most authors and most subjects — be said to have given us the last word on Stalin as man rather than monster. Allan Bullock may have the final say: 'Hitler and Stalin were not monsters. They were men, and that's the horror of it.'

Barry Baldwin

Atomic Classic

Togzhan Kassenova, *Atomic Steppe: How Kazakhstan Gave Up the Bomb*, Stanford University Press, 2022, 384 pages, paperback ISBN 9781503632431, £22.99

Kazakhstan became a Soviet atomic heartland by providing the ideal field laboratory for nuclear war. For forty years, blasts echoed across the steppes in an uncanny soundtrack for the surrounding indigenous communities. The bombs were unstoppable, and the barbarism of Russian destruction knew no bounds. Kazakh ancestral homelands were polluted by ionising radiation, prominent artists and intellectuals were displaced, and those who presented resistance against military action were imprisoned. Exactly four hundred and fifty-six nuclear weapons were tested across Semipalatinsk Nuclear Test Site — the Polygon — between 1949 and 1989. Yet by 1993, the site had been jettisoned by the Russian Ministry of Defence and left to fester. So how did a post-Soviet nuclear state unshackle itself from the nuclear imperialist harms of Russia to become nuclear-free?

Atomic Steppe provides an account of this hidden history that is both agonising and elegant by turn. To understand the lives of Kazakh nuclear-affected communities, Kassenova undertook extensive archival research and conducted interviews with the people who live in the villages that surround the Polygon. She travelled to Karaul and Sarzhal, to Dolon, Chagan and beyond, to collect the narratives that are shared within *Atomic Steppe*. Her book paints a vivid and stark picture. It describes both the cultural heritage and natural beauty of Kazakhstan, and the aftermath of the atrocities that have been committed against Kazakh people, with precision and deep compassion. It also tells a story of ancestry, as Kassenova's deep connection to her own Kazakh heritage and homeland is made apparent. Small details of her own childhood spent in the Soviet Union add further humanity to this complex and compelling text.

Atomic Steppe is a book of two halves that have been fused together to create a perfect whole. The first half describes the legacy of Kazakhstan's Soviet nuclear weapon tests. Conversely, the second part explores Kazakhstan's subsequent independence and the rugged pathway towards its emergence as a nuclear-free state in the early 1990s. Kassenova provides nuance and insight as she describes the complex and sometimes messy process of denuclearisation. Her extensive research provides hitherto unwritten insights into how Kazakhstan became nuclear-free. For example, the diplomatic context and processes behind the removal of nuclear weapons and the destruction of missile silos are described meticulously. It is this attention to detail that makes *Atomic Steppe* brilliant as it draws together the threads of a multifaceted nuclear story. It is completely unique, an absolute must-read, and it will become an atomic classic of our time.

Becky Alexis-Martin

History, which will not go away

Colm Tóibín, *The Magician*, Viking 2021, 438 pages, £18.99, ISBN 9780241004616

Colm Tóibín, *Vinegar Hill*, Carcanet 2022, 144 pages, £12.99, ISBN 9781800171619

Inner lives have always been at the forefront of Colm Tóibín's writing: the world impinges as it will, but it's a fictional character's, or a fellow novelist's growth into selfhood in all its 'complexity and ambiguity and secrecy', as he says of Henry James, against which he tests all the resources of his art. James in *The Master* (2004), in this regard, was relatively easy prey given the perfect laboratory conditions of 1895-9, Tóibín's chosen focus, and of his withdrawal, after the failed premiere of *Guy Domville*, from the social whirl of the capital – from contemporary history as such – to the closeted remoteness of Lamb House in Rye. *The Master* grants James one geopolitically compromised outing as a hanger-on at the court of the Brits in Ireland, navigating a nervous passage between Dublin Castle and the Royal Hospital at Kilmainham, and reigniting memories of the countrywide 'squalor both abject and omnipresent ... hostile stares and dark accusing eyes' of a previous visit to Cork, the 'sullenness of the Irish' which now pursues him 'right up to the castle gates.'. The remainder of the novel takes up residence among the griefs, nostalgias, dreams and sexual yearnings of James' belated reckoning with his own stalled creativity, or what Tóibín calls the imponderable forces at work in the 'great white blankness of the unconscious mind'. The homoerotic subplot has James' retreat into the 'defiantly miniscule and unportentous' reach its apogee in an artistic stand-off between his increasingly baroque, introverted texts and the leaping ambition of Hendrick Andersen's World City of international harmony:

tragedy repeated as farce. He departs the novel looking more than ever like Marcher in 'The Beast in the Jungle', 'a man of his time, *the* man, to whom nothing on earth was to have happened' — Tóibín's point about this resemblance, made elsewhere, reads 'nothing' in exclusively sexual terms, but 'of his time' and 'on earth' connote an even larger absence, however distantly.

As if picking up where *The Master* and *Love in a Dark Time's* selected encounters with the 'secret dotted line that runs right through Western literature' left off, *The Magician* makes relatively short work of Thomas Mann's unconsummated fantasy life transferred to his fictions, as it suggests the author himself did. Mann's exit from Europe in 1939 to the last flight from Malmö and the *SS Washington* finds him momentarily preoccupied:

'As he lifted his head and looked out at the vast expanse of water, names came to him, and then faces – Armin Martens blushing, Willri Timpe standing naked, Paul Ehrenberg leaning towards him earnestly, Klaus Heuser's soft lips ... Katia and Erika approached; Katia asked him what he was thinking about. "The book," he said [*Lotte in Weimar*, where Goethe's arousal on waking derives, in part, from the 'glowing vigorous arm' of a 'handsome huntsman'], "If I could get this section right."

What Tóibín and Mann, are after is a comprehensive *erkenntnis*, knowledge, psychological understanding, realisation – as far as that were possible — of the social and intellectual experiences informing every stage of the German writer's profoundly serious and world-conscious art, in a narrative that runs seamlessly from his roots in Hanseatic Lübeck's cultural conservatism and patrician civic duty all the way to the novel's neatly symmetrical ending: the return from exile to his father's graveside in that city and to the music of Buxtehude in the reconstructed *Dom*, a tentative but irreducible affirmation of the German values ('The secret is called Beauty') he's spent his whole life defending.

Tóibín has spoken of his trepidation at the prospect of all the 'epic material', political and philosophical, inseparable from any meaningful engagement with a protagonist more wedded to the public sphere than any in his fictions to date. But his understated, fluid, scene-shifting prose – 'The reader has a right to say, Get on with a story,' – emerges as the perfect foil to Mann's portentousness: the next sentence after the Buxtehude – 'He asked the driver to wait for him while he had hot chocolate and a marzipan tart in one of the nearby cafés' – reminds one of the constant rebuffs administered in the course of the novel to their disciplinarian, intellectually self-aggrandizing father by hedonistic, transgressive Klaus and Erika; or of Klaus's inability, in *The Children's Story* (1925), to free up his version of an idealised, precocious childhood without first killing off the head of the family and placing his death mask, 'mounted on black velvet', on the wall above Mama's bed, 'with his severe but serene smile ... dreaming into the early hours of the morning his deadly earnest dreams'.

The Magician draws freely upon the contents of Mann's novels and stories, their resounding achievement, masterpiece piled on masterpiece, never in doubt – Tóibín has never displayed any anxiety of influence in relation to his literary forebears. The final work, *Felix Krull*, finds Mann mediating as Tóibín recounts it on aspects of the human condition – 'not ever [to] be trusted ... they could reverse their own story as the wind changed ... their lives – a continuous, enervating and amusing effort to appear plausible' – that pertain more to his tortuous career as a polemicist: the virulent warmongering of *Reflections of a Non-Political Man*, wrong-footed in 1918 by Germany's ignominious defeat and given, one suspects, a wide berth by Tóibín (who can read such a thing?): his grudging endorsement of the Republic's fledgling democracy, naïve optimism (wrong-footed again) and protracted reluctance, until 1933, to denounce Hitler: the scramble to exile and extensive lecture tours and radio broadcasts cementing his commitment to a universal humanism; the flirtations with American power – tea with Mrs Roosevelt during the siege of Stalingrad – and the Cold War status quo in both camps, vying to purchase his acquiescence. Mann as a creature of the calamitous zeitgeist, flailing in all directions, for the most part ensconced in the trappings of a refined and privileged lifestyle, could easily seem a disconsolate, shambolic figure, were it not for the moral imperative the novel shows driving him on at every turn. *This* seriousness, one feels, has something urgent to say about the role of the intellectual and of literature we had arguably lost sight of in a corner of the world that imagined itself – until the war in Ukraine, and countless indicators of a resurgent fascism to the contrary – set on a happier course. The convulsion identified by the *Reflections* – 'the agitation of everything calm ... the shaking of all cultural foundations' – and its outcome half a century later, as Mann takes in the reality of Buchenwald's transformation into a Soviet internment camp – 'No poems about love, or nature, or man, would ever serve to rescue this place from the curse that had descended on it' – speak directly to some of our innermost fears.

One turns with relief to the poems of *Vinegar Hill*, products of the blithe

interim when the ancient and modern horrors had receded and one could
convert the massacre of the Wexford United Irishmen in 1798, *pace*
Heaney, into a multi-layered canter through the painterly qualities of the
landscape, like Cézanne approaching Mont Sainte-Victoire from different
angles, the clouds conducting a balletic, 'dreamy' re-enactment of what, on
the fateful day, took place. In similar fashion, 'Tiepolo' draws our attention
away from a crucifixion scene rendered by the artist's son to the way
'Clouds breeze in / And stay put, as though / Summoned by the painter /
Who did not want any more / Turbulence than was / Necessary'. There's a
winning, unforced playfulness on every page, an undertow certainty of
loss, lengthening shadows and personal mortality ('Dripping water and the
smell of darkness ... Don't follow me further. Move away, / Don't follow
me further'), but never at the expense of the 'I will steer / Tomorrow on a
different course' which is Tóibín's quintessential restlessness and
productivity, each poem a momentary bystander caught on the point of
disappearing. Or it's history that, repeatedly, occupies that position,
tweaked aside even as it comes within hailing distance, like the 'Troops
gathering' three months before the outbreak of the Spanish Civil War in
perhaps the lightest squib of the collection, 'Anton Webern in Barcelona',
or 'Arafat in Tunis', less worthy of memory's wandering attention than the
sexual allure of his entourage, 'a dozen young men in leather jackets / And
tight jeans ... I wondered what they did when darkness fell ... Was one of
them a favourite, or two?' The tweaking, of course, works both ways: a
visit to the White House for St Patrick's Day is curtailed by the 'soft
power, soft coercion' of a line of waiters emptying the room of its
occupants by 'push[ing] us firmly / Into timeless night'; a poem that
celebrates Emily Kngwarreye's powerful art remapping the aboriginal
homeland in contrast to Enniscorthy's muted identity and the 'Tentative,
unbrave, reticent' Dublin sky, reaches much the same conclusion – 'The
world lives in history / While we, poor lost ones, / Wither in time'.

Stephen Winfield

Momentum

Monica McWilliams, *Stand Up, Speak Out: My life working for women's rights, peace and equality in Northern Ireland and beyond*, Blackstaff Press, 2021, 368 pages, hardback ISBN 9781780733227, £19.99

This thorough, informative and insightful autobiography is compulsive reading for anyone interested in how 'the Peace Process' in Northern Ireland led to an international agreement signed by the leaders of the British and Irish governments, Tony Blair and Bertie Ahern, on Good Friday, 1998.

Monica's is a woman's story of the violent years of the 'Troubles'. It is punctuated by personal descriptions of her childhood, a bright Catholic girl in Kilrea; at school; bearing two sons; juggling childcare, university research, and campaigning. With other community activists she worked for better recognition of domestic violence, whilst recognising how mothers struggled to steer older children away from paramilitary groups where they were in danger from kneecapping, serious injury or sudden death. She describes how her close friend Avila Kilmurray's reflections on vicious events would often turn not into thoughts of revenge but into moving poetry. I was struck by the effort she put into developing friendships and supportive women's networks amongst all communities.

Most descriptions of these years are written by men. The focus is on atrocities committed in the name of the IRA or loyalist groups; the continual tit-for-tat violence across the divided communities in the name of retribution. McWilliams tells the same stories, but with a woman's eye and ear, which makes it different. The message that a stop to killings requires an equally strong development of cross community decision making comes through far more strongly as a result.

It takes someone who was born and brought up in Northern Ireland to describe the strength of the cultural labelling that was part of their daily life from the day they were born and then went to school. A simple home address or previous school could rule a youngster in or out of a job. Monica was a young woman as she 'joined the thousands who walked to Belfast City Hall on 2nd February 1992 to demand the "right to live free from intimidation and violence",' yearning for a non-sectarian future life for her young children.

Monica saw clearly that a focus on violent atrocities alone led to

108   *Our Common Security*

pressure indeed for decommissioning of all firearms but left out the need for an equally essential creation of constitutional politics to promote general diversity, inclusivity and equality. *Stand Up, Speak Out* emphasises how official talks started between the two governments behind the scenes much earlier and accelerated when John Major took over from Thatcher, and Patrick Mayhew became Secretary of State. He made a ceasefire the requirement that only parties which had complied could be at the talks. Monica describes how,

'she felt a cloud lifting as the IRA declared the "complete cessation of military operations in order to enhance the democratic process" as TV news showed a cavalcade of cars draped in Irish tricolours blasting their horns as they drove about West Belfast, whereas leaders on the unionist side were the opposite of joyful, with dire warnings of impending turmoil, with Jim Molineaux, the leader of the UUP [Ulster Unionist Party], describing the ceasefire as "destabilising" for unionism.'

She felt 'baffled' and was very relieved when, two months later, the leading paramilitaries from the more working class loyalist areas 'David Ervine, Plum (William) Smith, Gary McMichael and Gusty Spence sat together under the umbrella of the Combined Loyalist Military Command to announce their ceasefire, and expressed "abject and true remorse" for the suffering on the group's behalf'.

The scene was set for McWilliams to help transform these community-based women's networks into an organisation that would be listened to in the political talking that was to follow. The task was huge.

'Avila had worked out that the new electoral system allowed for ten parties to be at the talks, a women's party might be able to reach the threshold for admission if it won enough votes across Northern Ireland. Bronagh Hinds contacted a Northern Ireland official to enquire what the position would be if a new party wished to stand. "Stunned" silence was followed by the question, "What Party?" Bronagh replied "A women's party", and asked for time to consult about a name.

Once Northern Ireland Women's Coalition (NIWC) had a name, it set about finding enough candidates to stand under its agreed programme of three principles: 'Inclusion, Human Rights, and Equality'. Monica describes how:

'... the final list of 70 names was like a mosaic: there were women from all classes and every part of Northern Ireland, rural as well as urban. We came from Catholic, republican, nationalist traditions as well as Protestant, loyalist and unionist backgrounds; worked in the home, in business, trade unions, in all tiers of education and in public service. This was the type of diversity we wanted; It was the cumulative voice across the country that would allow two representatives to be at the table.'

The brilliant teamwork of this effort was astounding. *Stand Up, Speak Out* celebrates each and every moment. The clock was ticking and nearly beat them as they delivered their registration papers to May Blood at the electoral office with only a minute to spare.

By then a framework had been set as the two governments agreed to invite George Mitchell from the US Congress to oversee the talks, while General John de Chastelain from Canada and former Prime Minister Harri Holkeri from Finland were asked to lead an international body on arms commissioning which would work in parallel with the peace talks. The women's lobby, therefore, and its two tier goal of a peaceful future alongside inclusivity, human rights and equality were established from the start. In addition the whole process had become international.

The next chunk of *Stand Up, Speak Out* brings back vivid memories for me, because a couple of days after the 1997 general election, on 1st May, Mo Mowlam asked if I would be her PPS (Parliamentary Private Secretary) and take on an additional task to liaise with women in their communities, which I eagerly agreed to. 'We can't do it, Helen, without the women's support' she said at our first meeting, on returning from her first visit to Belfast as Secretary of State, 'so do the Parliamentary stuff here, but get over there as much as you can to meet the women'. More importantly, it gives new insight into the fascinating day-by-day retelling of intense debate and diplomacy, homophobic insults, new friendships across the community divides, disruptive violence over parades, and compromises to make it work. *Stand Up, Speak Out* is riveting to read, and because it is riddled with Monica's reminiscences of how she was able to combine her children's school activities with meetings, international events, politics and very tense moments, it brings a new perspective into the ensuing intense dramatic year that led to the Good Friday Agreement on 10th April 1998, the referendum on 21st June giving the Agreement public endorsement and, finally, the election of a devolved Legislative Assembly sitting at Stormont on 1st July 1998. All this took place just 11 days before the start of the Orange Order marches on 12th July. Mo's favourite phrase over this period was 'momentum' and, indeed, it was that speed and momentum that brought success.

Throughout the book, McWilliams analyses and picks out special moments which threatened the whole process but also those where careful and skilful diplomacy won through. For example, the Women's Coalition, intensely aware that the campaign did not stop with the Agreement, knew that a strong 'Yes' campaign had to be fought and won at each and every community meeting they attended. The same urgency and buzz that formed the NIWC was indeed fundamental to the 75% 'YES' result in the north.

Belfast's 'Good Friday Agreement' is a lasting tribute to how women and local communities should be at the heart of peace building. It is used as a fine example around the world. McWilliams autobiography is an important illustration of why that is the case. It expounds why and how the pain of violent enmity and destructive acts can be transformed into political dialogue and debate when human rights, diversity and equality become normal rules of decision making.

However, as McWilliams moves on to her role on the Assembly and, later, as a Human Rights Commissioner we become increasingly aware of how painstakingly slow that process can be. Full implementation of the basic principle that cross community dialogue and equal treatment, rather than angry remonstration, remains 'work in progress'. It is sad that the problems raised by leaving the European Union, which played such an important role in delivering the Agreement, are still making the future of a devolved Legislative Assembly in Stormont shaky.

So perhaps the title of the final chapter of this book will be part of the answer: *From the Local to the Global: Sharing the Learning*. Power-sharing has worked. Monica tells how grief was shared by community leaders at the funerals of former military activists such as David Ervine or Martin McGuinness. There is at a community level, and perhaps particularly amongst women, a strong desire to find solutions to current crises in the world such as climate change, health, and the cost of living, rather than returning to a sectarian past. Monica McWilliam's autobiography sets out the continuing goals.

Productive Borderline

Allen Ellenzweig, *George Platt Lynes: The Daring Eye*, Oxford University Press, 639 pages, hardback, ISBN 9780190216666, £25.99

Having read David Leddick's *Intimate Companions* (2000), a group biography of the photographer George Platt Lynes, the painter Paul Cadmus and the impresario Lincoln Kirstein ('and their circle'), I imagined we had all the life we needed of George Platt Lynes; but Ellenzweig's 639 pages make their own persuasive case to the contrary. Ellenzweig speaks of Lynes having been 'raised in the bosom of rectory-tude' in the family home (p.360). His father was an Episcopal minister who had trained as a lawyer. Both parents seem to have accepted their son's homosexuality and, to some extent, the other men it brought into their orbit, with equanimity. They also tended to indulge his profligacy, helping out whenever he got himself into financial difficulties, even after the Wall Street Crash of 1929. Indeed, his was a lifetime of being constantly bailed out, first by his parents, then by his younger brother, Russell, who once said of him, 'George begins to prosper, and from then on he's broke' (p.242). Ellenzweig speaks of 'a modus operandi that was to characterize the rest of his life—enlisting others to help support him in a style of life he could just barely afford' (p.203). Lynes would learn that, even if not rich, you could get access to riches: the privileges of wealth were available second-hand if you were already blessed—as he was—with the privileges of beauty, sociability, and *nerve*.

When Lynes went to Paris in 1925 at the age of eighteen, his eyes were opened not only to modernism but also to a public homosexual subculture of a kind he had not experienced before. For instance, he visited the Strix, 'a queer place', as he called it, with a mixed crowd: tables with only men, others with only women, and others still with both. In an enthusiastic letter to a student friend back home, he wrote: 'Nothing violent happened: there was no demonstration of any kind. Only exuberance. Yet two men (well over forty) who sat at a table next to me spoke long and loud using very often the word homosexual' (p.36). The lack of violence or demonstration confirmed the sophistication of Paris.

From the start, Lynes was strategically ingratiating when it came to the development of useful relationships. But many encounters developed into genuine friendships. It is clear, for instance, that Gertrude Stein and Alice B. Toklas, who could be formidably standoffish to those who tried to come within the compass of their lives, were soon very fond of Lynes; as he of them. It is no wonder that he made such remarkable portraits of the two women. Moreover, while there are many instances of bad behaviour on his part—one that stands out is his much later attempt to steal Don Bachardy from Christopher Isherwood—he was able to rein himself in when he had to. Great tact was required, of course, in his professional life. Not many young men could so productively have managed sittings with such grand figures as André Gide and Thomas Mann, or even with the more modestly diffident E.M. Forster.

Photography was less a vocation than a contingent expediency: Lynes's first ambition had been to make it as a modernist writer. He also tried running a bookshop before turning to the camera. He began as a portraitist, and was quick to recognise that his career would make stronger headway if he chose subjects who were well-known, or getting to be so: he could hitch a ride on their fame. He later branched out from portraiture, becoming a sensitive and inventive photographer of ballet dancers, in particular for Lincoln Kirstein and George Balanchine's American Ballet (later the New York City Ballet); and when feeling the need to develop more commercial skills, he moved into fashion shoots for *Harper's Bazaar*, *Town and Country*, and *Vogue*. Less publicly, he also specialised in nude images of men, a genre in which he was to become a great pioneer.

In 1927, Lynes had met a couple, Glenway Wescott and Monroe Wheeler, eventually a writer and an arts administrator (at the Museum of Modern Art in New York) respectively. Wheeler slept with, and then fell in love with, him. The following year he joined them in the south of France. The relationship became triangular, though not equilaterally: poor Wescott was somewhat edged to one side, even though the three of them lived together for more than a decade. As Ellenzweig rightly comments, 'these three men designed a way of life that appears as inventively bohemian as the roundelay of London's Bloomsbury Group' (p.10).

In 1946, Lynes moved to Hollywood, where he found many more celebrities who, notwithstanding their fame, craved even more images of themselves and could pay to assuage the craving. He said of Tinseltown: 'This is the most homosexual, and of course anti-homosexual town in the world' (p.404). Any gay American in the post-war period had to perform a delicate balancing act on the tightrope between those two cultures.

Lynes's relationship with Alfred Kinsey in the 1950s 'supplied moral and material support' (p.422). Kinsey was an admirer of his art and helped him, both morally and financially, by acquiring many of his photographs for the Kinsey Institute's archives at the University of Indiana. Lynes, though, was concerned both that the images might vanish into the vaults never to be seen again by members of the public, and that they might be regarded as pornography. Kinsey tried to reassure him on both counts. They also worked out ways of transferring the images to the institute at Bloomington without putting them in the mail, for which they could have been prosecuted.

When the swagger of abstraction held sway in the galleries and salesrooms of New York, times were especially hard for gay artists. On this point, Ellenzweig quotes the art historian James Saslow: 'The triumph of abstract art set back gay expression by rigorously excluding any narrative subject' (p.272). Photography, of course, is predominantly a representational art; so gay photography may be said to have found itself well out on a limb. Commenting on the fact that, on a visit to the Grand Canyon, Lynes left his camera in its case ('It's totally without human scale,' he said), Ellenzweig writes: 'George's artistic project was a human one: the face, the body, the gesture, the dance figure in posed but frozen motion, nude figures in relation to each other' (p.385). It was a project whose warmth and sensitivity is properly recognised by Ellenzwieg's account of the life that made the work.

Both scholarly and gossipy, this book has a cast of hundreds (Bertrand Russell's fourth wife Edith Finch makes several fleeting guest appearances), but Ellenzweig marshals his material with a steady hand. I have just one complaint. As far as I can recall, only once, and only fleetingly, does he acknowledge Lynes's failures: 'To be sure, in his imaginative exploration of different ways to present men naked, there were failed efforts, such as a few Camp conceits that seem laughable' (p.423). This is a pity. The phrase 'Camp conceits' could mean anything, 'Camp' itself being such a flexible term and such a subjective valuation, it seems to me that the detail of such laughable conceits could tell us a great deal about Lynes's aesthetic. After all, the very best of his work is itself far from being un-Camp. I would have liked to know more about his negotiation of the narrow line between failure and success in this respect, and how he himself made such judgements about his own work.

One of the book's illustrations shows Jean Cocteau, Cecil Beaton, Glenway Wescott and George Platt Lynes on a jaunt to Coney Island in 1936. Ellenzweig presents it as being emblematic: 'Here were the Western world's gay male cultural forces meeting in a moment of high levity ... Whatever social restraints they may have lived under in England, France, and America, each one contributed, by his personal demeanor and by his art, to an easing of restrictions on the border between public and private homosexuality' (p.250). That borderline was one of the most productive locations of twentieth-century cultural development.

Gregory Woods

THE ROSARY

I was hitch-hiking
From Gorey back to Enniscorthy
One Sunday night in summer.
I had been drinking vodka,
And was a bit surprised when
The family who picked me up
Said the Rosary, mystery
By mystery, one leading,
The rest following.

The car drove south to the sound
Of sober prayer: One Our Father
Ten Hail Marys, One Glory Be.
To be repeated five times
(The Rosary is repetitious)
And then comes the Hail Holy Queen.
By then we were past Ferns.
It would not be long
Before we reached Enniscorthy.

Colm Tóibín
Vinegar Hill

END INFO

European
Nuclear
Disarmament

@ENDInfo_
endinfo.net

Published by
the *Bertrand
Russell Peace
Foundation*

END Info was launched in March 2019 to aid the work of the Bertrand Russell Peace Foundation in response to the collapse of the Intermediate-range Nuclear Forces Treaty and the attendant nuclear risks. The Russell Foundation and *END Info* played an important role in building the 'Nuke Free Europe' network (nukefreeeurope.eu), which brings together a range of peace organisations for a joint campaign to rid the continent of all nuclear weapons. In the following pages you will find a selection of articles from issues 28 - 31 of the newsletter. To receive this and future issues, contact tomunterrainer@russfound.org.

* * * * *

Nuclear Ukraine
END Info

Up until the dissolution of the USSR, Ukraine hosted about a third of all Soviet nuclear weapons. Following a 1991 referendum, where an overwhelming proportion voted for independence, the fate of these Soviet weapons was in the hands of the Commonwealth of Independent States. Ukraine was a 'founder' of the CIS but did not actually join after declining to sign the CIS Charter in 1993.

It was not until 1994 that Ukraine formally agreed to dismantle the 'left behind' nuclear weapons system. That same year it signed the Non-Proliferation Treaty and renounced nuclear weapons possession for good.

Nuclear weapons possession was firmly and quite rightly renounced in 1994 but nuclear power has been an enduring feature of Ukraine's infrastructure. The risks and hazards of nuclear power have been well documented, not least in the recent Spokesman Dossier titled *Nuclear Power?* But the people of Ukraine have no need for book-length summaries of the potentially deadly consequences of nuclear power for in the north of the country, on the Belarus border, sits Chernobyl. Such peace-time risks have now been joined by the acute risks of nuclear power in times of war. As Jan Vande Putte, co-author of a recent Greenpeace study, points out: "For the first time in history a major war is being waged in a country with multiple nuclear reactors and thousands of tons of highly radioactive spent fuel". The Greenpeace study (02/03/22) focuses on severe nuclear hazards at just one of Ukraine's nuclear power sites: the Zaporizhzhia plant, which with six nuclear reactors is the largest such plant in the whole of Europe. The study sets out the risks:

"In a worst-case scenario, where explosions destroy the reactor containment and cooling systems, the potential release of

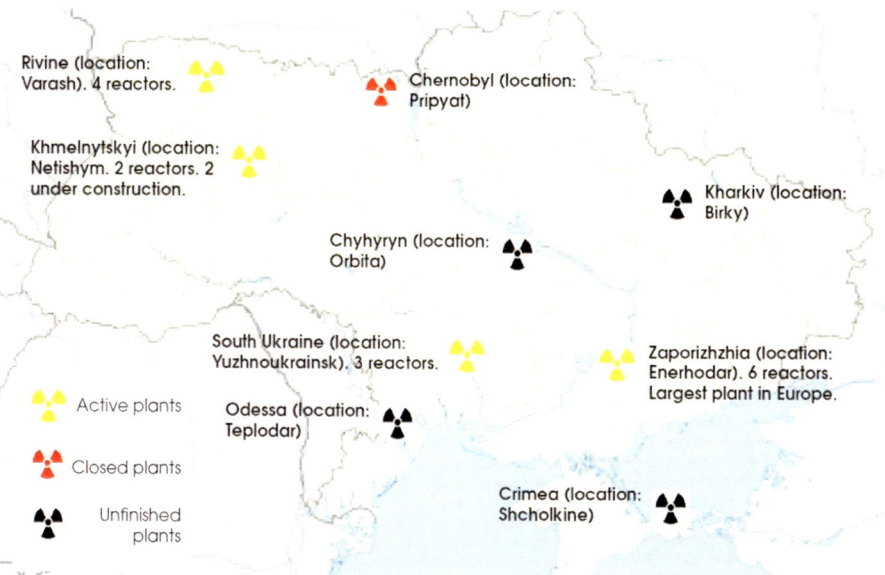

radioactivity from both the reactor core and spent fuel pool into the atmosphere could create a disaster far worse than (at Fukushima) ... with areas of land hundreds of kilometres from the reactor site potentially becoming inhospitable for decades. Even without direct damage to the plant, the reactors rely on the electric grid for operating cooling systems, on the availability of nuclear technicians and personnel and access to heavy equipment and logistics."

If Putin's invasion of Ukraine and his subsequent nuclear threats weren't bad enough - and they are very bad indeed - then the prospect of nuclear disaster, either deliberate or accidental, compounds an already awful situation.

If those who attempt to maintain some form of safety at the Chernobyl site are prevented from doing so, if supplies are cut off, if shifts cannot change or similar then Putin will have yet more death and destruction to account for. If a single shell or missile 'accidentally' hits just one reactor at one of the active plants then the consequences could be immense. If electricity supplies are disrupted and cooling systems fail, then nuclear-meltdown and all that means could unfold. These are risks of waging 'conventional war' in places with nuclear power plants. The world knows all of the risks of nuclear power but has failed to act. Will it take another 'unthinkable' disaster like Chernobyl to force the issue? We must hope that it doesn't.

Meanwhile, as energy supplies are impacted as a consequence of

Putin's actions, there will be many who rush towards nuclear power as a means of 'energy independence'. Such a rush is misjudged on many levels - not least the questions of timescale and interdependence of nuclear fuel supply - but it will be fundamentally misjudged because nuclear power is dirty, dangerous and - as can be seen from events in Ukraine - potentially deadly.

From END Info 30.

* * * * *

End this war
Tom Unterrainer

It is not possible to fully capture the appalling dimensions of a war by listing grim statistics. If such statistics made a difference to those who control the armies and institutions that wage war, then millions slaughtered in wars, large and small, over past decades would not have perished. The disturbing truth is that human life means little to war-makers. A different class of mathematical object matters much more to such people: the calculus of power.

We are the opposite of war-makers. We aim for peace and strive to remove all roadblocks to it. So in reckoning with the calamities produced by President Putin's invasion of Ukraine, we absorb the grim statistics. The UN Office of the High Commissioner for Human Rights reports that between 4am on the morning of 24 February 2022 and midnight on 12 April 2022, civilian casualties totalled: "485 men, 313 women, 31 girls, and 54 boys, as well as 72 children and 977 adults whose sex is yet unknown". 1,932 corpses. In addition, many thousands of men, women, boys, girls and children have suffered injuries of which many will be life-changing. The report comments:

> Most of the civilian casualties recorded were caused by the use of explosive weapons with a wide impact area, including shelling from heavy artillery and multiple launch rocket systems, and missile and air strikes.

Added to the civilian deaths are those of the 'combatants'. According to Ukrainian, Russian and NATO estimates, thousands on each side have died in the fighting. Both Russian and Ukrainian forces include conscript fighters.

To these numbers should be added all those who have died in the eight years of fighting in Eastern Ukraine/Donbass between 2014-2022 and all those yet to be slaughtered. As in all wars, the death toll only ever increases. This war must end.

In a 1964 letter to German social psychologist and humanist philosopher Erich Fromm, Bertrand Russell argued that: "War should be treated as murder is treated. It should be regarded with equal horror and with equal aversion." War is organised murder. The organisers of murder together with the individual murderers richly deserve our collective horror and aversion.

In the case of the war in Ukraine, international legal procedures have been initiated to catalogue the crimes already committed and to document those that will come if the war continues. Tribunals and hearings are under preparation. The leaders of NATO member states have been very clear in describing the horrors of the war in Ukraine and in identifying a culprit. Yet Mr Biden, Mr Johnson and allies are less forthcoming in their denunciations of the wars, some of them 'illegal', waged by US, British and NATO forces. Mr Johnson is vocal on crimes in Ukraine but silent on crimes in Yemen, a horror-show of human suffering imposed on that country by Britain's ally, Saudi Arabia, and fuelled by arms sales from the UK. Mr Biden sees horror in Ukraine but sees nothing wrong with the wars he supported over decades of 'public service'.

As bad as this rank hypocrisy is, the stark fact is that the US, UK and allies in the nuclear-armed NATO alliance are already preparing for the next war. Peace, justice and human rights are not actually on their agenda.

The next war

Without doubt, ultimate responsibility for the war in Ukraine rests with Mr Putin. It would, however, be untrue to say that each and every opportunity to de-escalate was taken. *END Info* and other publications traced the facts of these failures and documented the troubling developments that went with them. We argued for alternative measures: real security and cooperation, denuclearisation and a nuclear-free-zone in Europe. We advocated for diplomacy rather than brinkmanship. In so doing, we echoed the calls of the peace movements throughout the 60s, 70s, 80s and 90s, when opportunities for a comprehensive change of course seemed credible afterer the dissolution of the Warsaw Pact. Rather than taking steps to achieve real security, NATO expanded both geographically and in terms of posture. NATO is now a 'global' force with an ever-expanding area of operation.

Despite the growing risks, 2021 seemed like a year of real possibilities compared to today. In 2021 we witnessed widespread discussion in Germany on the future of US nuclear bombs stationed in that country under NATO agreements. We witnessed some NATO member states agreeing to send observers to the First State Parties meeting of the Treaty on the Prohibition of Nuclear Weapons. Think-tanks and trade unions were actively engaged in developing a new approach to common security. Everything has shifted in a deadly direction.

It is common knowledge and common sense that all wars and military conflicts end in diplomacy and negotiation. Even where 'military victory' at the expense of murder, death and destruction is 'achieved' by one side or another, diplomacy and negotiation conclude the matter. It will likely be the case that the horrors in Ukraine will end in a similar fashion. Everyone knows this, yet those in power do not have the good sense to act on this basis. Rather, they are preparing for the next war.

For example, just three days after Russia's invasion of Ukraine, a referendum in neighbouring Belarus approved a new constitution that ditched the country's non-nuclear-weapon status (27 February 2022). According to reports, 65.2% of those who voted agreed to this change, which makes it possible, for example, for Russia to deploy nuclear weapons in Belarus. No doubt, Mr Lukashenko will tell the people of Belarus that such a move 'enhances our security'. Such a turn of phrase will be familiar to the peoples of Finland and Sweden, two countries which look set to join the NATO nuclear-armed alliance to 'enhance security'. If it's true that the Belarus decision has made the world a more dangerous place, then it is also true that Finland and Sweden joining NATO makes the world a more dangerous place.

Military 'solutions' are nothing of the sort, they just bring greater risks and a greater possibility of death and destruction. 'Security' is not enhanced with nuclear weapons or by joining a nuclear-armed alliance. Rather than achieving 'security', risks are multiplied and the foundations for the next war are established.

Militarisation

Preparations for the next war can be detected not only in the serial failures to pursue peace, the geographic expansion of NATO, the development of new nuclear weapons and the rest. Europe is now entering a period of rapid re-militarisation. If we wind the clock back a year or two, we will recall President Trump's repeated complaints about the lack of military spending by European states. Trump has departed the political scene and we should hope that he never returns. However, Trumpian levels of military spending are now on the agenda.

As social conditions in Europe spiral ever downwards, as the prospect of widespread poverty intensifies, as living costs skyrocket and as the impacts of Covid and the deficiencies of the economy endure, European countries are pledging billions in increased military spending. Trump would be proud. These things cannot be isolated from the growth of right-wing political forces across the continent: from the Johnson government in Britain, through the streets and voting booths of France, to the government of Hungary. The situation is dangerous. Billions of Euros for machines of murder and destruction whilst the poor get poorer will not 'guarantee security'. Quite the opposite.

The dimensions of this crisis are not limited to developments in Europe. Note the already-shifting remit of the 'AUKUS' alliance between Australia, the UK and US. Within the past month, it has been announced that this alliance will now cover the development and deployment of hypersonic missiles. For what purpose? Who will be the target? Additionally, further efforts have been initiated to include Japan in the alliance. Such a move would massively escalate existing tensions in the region and would mark a significant change in military posture for Japan.

The arc of militarisation extends across the Atlantic, over Europe and far into the southern hemisphere. Existential risks follow this same arc.

End this war ... stop the next one
The peace movements face a monumental challenge as a result of Putin's war and the militarism of NATO and Europe. There are visible tensions and sharp disagreements. We are, however, united by an understanding that the immediate tasks are to end the war in Ukraine, end the death and destruction that come with it and to resist the drives to escalation. We are also united by the aim of stopping anything like this happening again. To achieve our aims, we must be clear-sighted about the longstanding dynamics and the more recent, dramatic, shifts. We must understand the potential consequences and prepare to resist them.

From END Info 31

* * * * *

Europe is militarising
Ludo De Brabander

What came before
NATO's relations with Ukraine date back to immediately after independence in 1991. The North Atlantic Alliance included the country in the North Atlantic Cooperation Council (1991) and the Partnership for Peace program (1994). From 1997, cooperation was deepened with the establishment of the NATO-Ukraine Commission (NUC). In 2008, the NATO summit in Bucharest decided that Ukraine could eventually become a member of the military alliance, without, however, opening the procedure for this (Membership Action Plan, MAP). Russia responded by labeling Ukraine's membership as a "red line." In 2009 the Euro-Atlantic military integration

of Ukraine was started through an 'Annual National Programme'.

Ukraine has been actively contributing to NATO military operations ever since. From then on, NATO also conducts annual multinational manoeuvres in Ukraine (under the name 'Rapid Trident') and in the Black Sea. The latter regularly take place off the coast of Crimea, which led to a serious incident last year between a British frigate and the Russian army, during which warning shots were fired. Moscow considers such military exercises 'provocations'. Secret British documents that were unintentionally made public show that scenarios of possible Russian reactions were calculated in advance.

Since the Warsaw summit (2016), NATO support to Ukraine has been provided through a 'Comprehensive Assistance Package'. In 2019, Ukraine's pursuit of NATO membership was constitutionally enshrined by Kiev. In 2020, Ukrainian President Zelensky approved the New National Security Strategy to further develop ties and integration with NATO into full membership.

Following the Russian annexation of Crimea and the outbreak of war in the Donbass region (2014), NATO responded with troop deployments, rising military budgets and arms supplies to Ukraine. That same year, at the summit in Wales, NATO heads of government agreed that member states' military budgets must be at least 2% of their Gross Domestic Product (GDP) by 2024. At that time, only Greece, the United Kingdom and the US reached that standard. Between 2015 and 2021, NATO's combined budgets grew by $155 billion.

The developments in Ukraine also have major repercussions for the Belgian military-budgetary trajectory. In 2017, the Swedish coalition decided to commit 9.2 billion euros in a program law for investments in weapons systems. The government is thus making an important concession to that other NATO standard of Wales, to set aside 20% of the military budget for military investment. In addition, the Michel government approved a defense growth path that should bring the military budget to 1.3% of GDP by 2030.

Belgium also responded to NATO by supplying around 300 soldiers to be stationed in Estonia and subsequently in Lithuania. They are part of the 4 multinational 'battlegroups' that the military alliance in Poland and the Baltic States developed in the context of the 'Enhanced Forward Presence', a decision of the NATO summit in Warsaw (2016).

In response to Russian military action in and around Ukraine, which eventually culminated in open war, NATO decided to increase its military presence in Eastern Europe. There are now 40,000 troops under

NATO command with another four new multinational battlegroups in Slovakia, Hungary, Bulgaria and Romania. Belgium pledged 300 troops to reinforce NATO's flank in Romania.

Military budgets are rising sharply

From the beginning of this year, European armaments and militarization gained momentum. Immense budget increases - until recently seen as unfeasible - are now becoming reality without significant debate.

In Belgium, at the end of January 2022, the government gave the green light to the STAR plan – 'Security, Technology, Ambition and Resilience' – which foresees that defense resources should increase to 1.54% of GDP by 2030. This includes a new investment plan worth more than 10 billion euros. The government approved a preliminary draft law for this at the end of February "for updating the military program law and the defense budget up to and including 2030". Additional costs have to be added to this for increasing the number of personnel from 26,000 to 29,000 and for the implementation of the POP plan (People-Our-Priority plan), which is intended to improve working conditions and the pay of the troops. Additional expenditure is also made for investments in infrastructure and in research and development of new technologies in collaboration with Belgian industry. The STAR plan reserves 1.8 billion euros for the latter.

Ultimately, the military budget is expected to amount to 6.9 billion euros in 2030, compared to 4.4 billion today. In reality, that could be even higher. In the run-up to the NATO meeting in Brussels at the end of March, the De Croo government has decided to allocate an additional 1 billion over the next three years for arms and ammunition stocks, protective equipment, anti-tank weapons, the vehicle fleet and IT and communication systems. This means that over a five-year period, a total of more than EUR 20 billion in military investments in weapon systems has been committed.

The same pattern can be seen in almost all NATO member states.

Immediately after the invasion, the German government announced that it would invest another 100 billion euros in the army this year. A growth path had already been mapped out for the German defense budget that was budgeted at 53 billion euros in 2022, an increase of 3.2% compared to the previous year. The war in Ukraine means that not since the defeat of the 'Third Reich', will so much money be invested in the military apparatus in such a short time. Chancellor Scholtz said his country would immediately increase its military budget to above 2% of GDP, up from 1.53% now.

In the Dutch coalition agreement of December 2021, it was already agreed that a structural additional 3 billion euros would be added for defense, to reach 1.85% of GDP in 2024. According to recent reports, the Rutte government is working on a plan to go to 2% of GDP in order to respond to a parliamentary motion that was passed with a large majority.

On March 16, the Italian parliament voted by a large majority to increase the military budget from 1.41% to 2% of GDP, or from 29.8 billion euros to 41 billion euros.

Although the US already spends astronomically high amounts on the military apparatus - almost 40% of global military expenditure - Washington is also planning another billion-dollar injection. US President Biden proposes increasing the military budget for the next fiscal year (starting this fall) to $813 billion, which would be an increase of $31 billion in one year.

French President Macron, who is in full electoral battle, has announced that the already planned increase in the military budget should be increased, without however giving details. According to the French military programming law (2019-2025), a strong budget increase is already foreseen. In 2025, military resources must be increased to 50 billion euros, compared to 41 billion euros this year. So probably a few billion more.

Spain, Denmark, Poland and Romania are also announcing major budget increases. Poland even wants to go to 3% of GDP next year (compared to 2.2% this year).

NATO member states together accounted for $1,049 billion in military expenditure in 2021. With the announced budget increases, many tens of billions will be added.

Russia's military budget is about $62 billion, which is 17 times less than NATO's military resources. Russia is unlikely to follow in the new arms race, as Moscow already spent 4.3% of GDP on military spending last year. With the sanctions on top, it looks like there's little margin left for further increases. This suggests that the military imbalance of power with NATO will become much greater. The question therefore arises as to why all these extra military resources are needed in the NATO member states? It seems that NATO is preparing for a possible new superpower confrontation. NATO defines not only Russia, but also China as a 'systemic rival'.

European 'Peace Facility' for Ukraine

A few days after the Russian invasion, the Council of the European Union decided to allow EUR 450 million worth of arms supplies to the Ukrainian army through the so-called 'peace facility' that came into effect at the end of March 2021. On March 23, 2022, the Council doubled the amount, so that eventually 900 million euros in arms can be supplied.

The Peace Facility was created to finance military missions and support to third countries under the EU's Common Security and Defense Policy (CSDP). The EUR 5 billion planned for the period 2021-2027 will be realized outside the EU budget. After all, according to the EU Treaty, expenditure in support of military operations must be financed with separate contributions from the Member States.

EU Member States have the right to supply weapons under the 'right of self-defence' provided for in Article 51 of the UN Charter. The 'Common Position', which regulates arms exports from the EU, also allows this in the context of self-defence. In contrast, both the Peace Facility and the Common Position impose restrictions. For example, arms transfers must not prolong or aggravate the conflict (Common Position criterion 3), which is difficult to assess in this existing war. Arms deliveries could greatly enhance the Ukrainian army's strike capability to bring a swift end to the war. Conversely, arms deliveries can effectively prolong and aggravate the conflict.

Criterion 7 states that the weapons must not fall into the hands of 'undesirable' end users. That could be Russian troops in the event that they overpower Ukrainian troops, weapons that are distributed to civilians, or weapons that end up with 'undesirable' militias when the fighting becomes 'unconventional'. In the event of Russian forces being expelled, such militias could target the Russian minority in the country or could be used to further fight the conflict with the insurgent republics (Luhansk and Donetsk).

Finally, criterion 2 states that the weapons may not be delivered if there is a risk that they will be used to commit serious violations of international humanitarian law. In addition to the reporting of Russian war crimes, there have already been reports of members of the Ukrainian army committing war crimes.

Similar provisions are also included in the Q&A of the European External Action Service which regulates arms transfers under the peace facility. However, the Council has not taken a public position on all these possible consequences of arms transfers. A concept note has been leaked that lists the above-mentioned risks, including restrictive measures, such as the provision that the weapons may not end up with entities other than the Ukrainian army. However, President Zelensky has stated at the start of the Russian aggression that Kiev will provide weapons to any civilian willing to fight.

Billions of arms deliveries to Ukraine

A large flow of weapons has been making its way to Ukraine since 2014, with the US as the main supplier. Between 2014 and 2021, the US provided at least $2.5 billion in weapons and military aid. More than $1 billion has been added since the Russian war. The Czech Republic, Poland, France, Turkey and the United Kingdom have also been supplying arms to the Ukrainian armed forces for several years, and it cannot be ruled out that they have been deployed against the insurgent rebel republics in the Donbass region.

Since the Russian invasion, arms deliveries have increased in intensity and volume. Most NATO member states (and some EU member states) have announced the delivery of defensive as well as offensive weapon systems. Belgium has stated that it will deliver 5,000 machine guns and 200 anti-tank weapons to the Ukrainian army.

The United Kingdom is one of the most active arms suppliers in this war, ranging from anti-tank and other missile systems, armored vehicles and artillery to associated ammunition. London is also committed to the delivery of eight naval vessels and a £1.7 billion frigate.

If you go over the list, you will arrive at hundreds of millions of euros in weapons and other military support.

Arms industry

Rising military budgets and massive military aid to Ukraine provide billions in revenue for the military industry. In January, a month before the outbreak of hostilities across Ukraine, US arms giants Raytheon and Lockheed Martin openly stated to their investors that the tensions "will make more business" for the arms companies. Raytheon supplies Stinger anti-aircraft missiles and together with Lockheed Martin the Javelin anti-tank missiles. Both companies are among the top five arms giants to have pumped $60 million into influencing US politics by 2020. In Washington, the arms industry employs 700 lobbyists, which is more than the number of Congressmen. At least 19 of those Congressmen have bought shares of both arms giants, some of them after the Russian invasion of Ukraine.

Even before the outbreak of large-scale hostilities, the global military industry was predicted to grow by 7% in 2022 (from $453 billion to $483 billion). Western Europe would become the fastest growing market according to these forecasts. The military bidding with rising budgets means that the predicted increase in turnover will turn out to be a serious underestimate. Two weeks after the invasion, arms companies' shares rose sharply. Shares of Raytheon rose by 8%, General Dynamics by 12%, Lockheed Martin by 18% and Northrop Grumman even by 22%. British BAE Systems saw its shares rise by 14% in the first week after the Russian invasion.

Rising military budgets and arms supplies are a boon to the arms industry, but are having negative repercussions on negotiations and diplomacy. If one side believes in military victory thanks to these deliveries, it could lead to a very bloody prolongation of the war in eastern Ukraine.

From END Info 31

* * * * *

Ukraine Negotiations

Joseph Gerson

Regardless of whether we agree with him or not, President Biden's statements that Vladimir Putin cannot remain in power and that Putin is a war criminal have compounded already complex negotiations to end Moscow's devastating and nationally self-defeating war of aggression.

Humanity will be sleepwalking to its doom unless the great powers negotiate nuclear disarmament, and to collaborate to stanch the climate chaos that haunts humanity's future.

With Russia's military advances in Ukraine stymied, and with the mounting death tolls, we are receiving contradictory reports about the state of Russian-Ukrainian diplomacy. Ukraine's lead negotiator Mykailo Podolyak reports that the negotiations with Moscow are "absolutely real", but that the Kremlin hasn't pulled back from its most ambitious war aims. Negotiations, he has said, could continue for months. Ukraine's Defense Intelligence, Brig. General Kyrylo Budanov is less optimistic, reporting that the negotiations are "vague and unpredictable". Turkey's President Erdogan, who has met with both the Russian and Ukrainian presidents in his efforts to mediate an end to the war, reports that negotiators have reached "understandings" about Ukraine and NATO, partial Ukrainian disarmament, collective security, and the use of the Russian language, but there have been no agreements on the future status of Crimea or the Donbas. And, contrary to Podolyak, the *New York Times* claims that Russia is signaling a change in its war goals, announcing that the "first stage of the operation" has been "mainly accomplished." While it "does not exclude continuing attacks on major Ukrainian cities, the *Times* reports that they are not Moscow's "primary objective". It contends that Russian forces will be concentrated on the "liberation of the Donbas."

Ukrainian and Russian lives will continue to be shattered until either a ceasefire or completion of successful negotiations are announced.

In recent months, I have been privileged to be a set of ears in a confidential series of track II discussions, initially designed to prevent the war and now to help frame diplomatic compromises that could end the bloodletting. Participants include former U.S., Russian and European officials—including military officers, advisors to their respective governments and scholars. A number of the participants communicate with their country's policy makers. A number of these people, despite their differences, have negotiated and otherwise worked together over many years. And even as emotions run high, the discourse is civil and "professional." While there could be unhappy professional consequences for some of the Western participants, one of the senior Russians has commented that "No new initiative comes without the risk of punishment."

This past week, as Ukrainian and Russian negotiators were meeting and other governments weighed in, one of these track II sessions was held to discuss the advocacy and dangers of a possible Western no-fly declaration, as well as what Ukrainian neutrality and disarmament would entail. With the exception of near unanimous opposition to the exceedingly dangerous possibility of a no-fly zone declaration, as described below, a range of possibilities were identified which hopefully will inform the diplomacy needed to end the war.

A No-Fly Zone and NATO "Peacekeepers"

While Russian forces grind away at Ukrainian resistance, there is glee in Washington that Moscow may have trapped itself in an Afghanistan-like quagmire. But one thing that thoughtful U.S. and Russian elites agree upon is that despite the ongoing negotiations, the situation may be as dangerous as during the Cuban Missile Crisis. Then the Kennedy Administration believed the odds were between a third and a half that the crisis would result in a thermonuclear exchange between the world's two most heavily armed nuclear powers.

Just as the United States has done at least thirty times during international crises and wars, Vladimir Putin has threatened the possible use of nuclear weapons and increased the alert status of his nuclear arsenal. In the words of former U.S. Strategic Command Chief, Admiral Charles Richard, the U.S. has used its strategic nuclear forces to "create the 'manoeuvre space' for us to project conventional military power strategically." This strategy works both ways. It has prevented the U.S. and NATO from establishing a no-fly zone over Ukraine to eliminate aerial support for Russian ground forces. As was the case during the Cuban missile crisis, nuclear alerts increase the danger of accidents, insubordinations, or miscalculations triggering the unimaginable. There are also fears that if the Russian military and President Putin find themselves on the defensive, in desperation Putin might fall back on attacking with chemical or low-yield nuclear weapons, risking escalation up the nuclear ladder.

Zelensky has repeatedly appealed for NATO to impose a no-fly zone, an appeal that has found resonance in Congress. Fortunately, thus far NATO leaders have bowed to the reality that enforcing a no-fly zone against Russia would inevitably trigger World War III, in the form of genocidal or omnicidal nuclear exchanges. Enforcing a no-fly zone would require attacking Russian anti-aircraft installations and shooting down Russian planes, to which Russia would respond in kind. Yet, in the track II discussion, a senior American warned that the longer the war continues, and as the Russian military is degraded, the temptation to impose a no-fly zone will grow.

A second reckless proposal, which was fortunately disregarded in Brussels, was made by Jaroslaw Kaczynski, Poland's president in the run up to the NATO summit. Standing beside Volodymyr Zelensky, he floated the idea of dispatching NATO "peacekeeping" forces, capable of defending themselves, to operate in Ukraine. His spokesman later elaborated that the operation would involve deploying NATO and other forces in regions of Ukraine that have yet to be occupied by Russia and protecting them "against further Russian activities".

In the track II session, a senior Russian advisor commented that "If Poland moves to impose a no-fly zone or otherwise intervenes in Ukraine, it will be considered an attack by a NATO member state." Similarly, immediately following the NATO summit, NATO leaders warned that if weapons of mass destruction were used within Ukraine, but their fallout drifted into NATO's territory, it could be interpreted an attack on NATO, necessitating military responses.

Neutrality & Demilitarization

Every war, for better or worse, ends with negotiations. While the details of Russian-Ukrainian negotiations remain tightly held secrets, track II participants assume that Russia's invasion will end with assurances that Ukraine will never join NATO and that it will become a neutral and significantly demilitarized state. Less certain is whether Moscow will insist on regime change in Kyiv in the guise of "denazification" or if Russia's territorial conquests will remain in place.

Russian ambitions in Ukraine, undefined as they continue to be, indicate that negotiating Ukrainian neutrality is at best a complex affair. As one Russian advisor commented, Moscow will insist that there be no possible military threats emanating from Ukraine for many decades to come. Recognizing the fragility of Swedish and Finnish neutrality, with both nations currently debating the possibility of applying for NATO membership, Russian leaders believe that neutrality cannot be rooted in what they perceive to be a hostile political environment. Thus, it is argued that meaningful agreements on Ukrainian neutrality will require progress in U.S-Russian and Russian-NATO negotiations, and they will need to be confirmed by an international treaty or United Nations Security Council resolution.

As if these obstacles are not sufficiently daunting, while Moscow states that regime change is not its goal, believing that neutrality must be rooted in a nation's political system and culture, it will demand some restructuring of the Ukrainian state, perhaps in the guise of its denazification demands. Not as difficult, but no slam dunk, are indications that Russia will demand intrusive inspections to verify Ukrainian neutrality and placing Kyiv's nuclear power plants under a special verification regime or in the future to be run by international operators.

Nonetheless, first steps in the direction of Ukrainian neutrality are being made. Under the pressure of Russia's invasion, President Zelensky has stated that, despite Ukraine's 2019 constitutional commitment to seeking NATO membership, he will not press the issue. He has stated that he is prepared to discuss neutrality as part of a peace deal with Russia but it needs to be guaranteed by third parties and approved in a referendum. It is possible that Zelensky may have wanted to opt for neutrality to prevent Russia's invasion, but political pressure from right-wing Ukrainian nationalist forces—including assassination threats—raised the political (and personal) costs of pursuing that option.

Regardless of how it is designed, Kyiv agreeing to becoming a neutral state will face significant Ukrainian political opposition necessitating strong support, and likely considerable input, from the United States and other NATO states.

There are, in fact, many forms of nation-state neutrality. Swedish, Austrian, Moldavan, Irish, and Swiss neutrality differ from one another. International law would require that Ukrainian neutrality, which prevailed between its 1990 independence until 2015, would require renunciation of Kyiv's ambitions to join NATO, a ban on the presence of foreign military troops and bases, the commitment to treat warring parties equally, and guarantees from a number of countries. Militarily, Ukraine would need the ability to defend its neutrality and territorial integrity. Whether this would include Donetsk, Luhansk, and other regions now controlled by the Russian military appears to be the most divisive issue. Ukraine would also be prohibited from taking part in any international miliary conflict, making its territory available to nations at war (as Cambodia did during the Vietnam War), and providing troops or mercenaries to forces at war.

Determining how Ukraine would defend its neutrality will require intense negotiations. Sweden maintains a professional military, reinforced by conscripts, and its military-industrial complex produces weapons for export as well as for national defense. Switzerland has universal male military service. And at the end of the neutrality spectrum is Ireland which spends little on its military and is widely believed to be unable to defend itself against possible aggression, theoretical though it may be. That said, a neutral Ukraine would require some form of police for domestic security, a border/customs patrol, and a minimal military. Determining where weapons and related training for these forces would come from implies further questions about orientation and influence, and would be another highly contested issue.

Guaranteeing Ukrainian neutrality raises other questions. President Zelensky has said that it would require guarantees from the United States and other NATO nations. Russians respond by asking how this would differ in substance from Ukraine formally joining NATO. There is also the reality that nothing, even constitutions and international treaties that guarantees they will endure. With the people of and governments of Sweden and Finland debating whether to end decades of neutrality and apply for membership in NATO Russian analysts are wondering how Ukrainian neutrality could be guaranteed.

What Then?

Ukrainian civilians and soldiers and Russian soldiers are being killed and maimed every day. Many of Ukraine's cities are being reduced to rubble. And indiscriminate sanctions are wreaking havoc and delivering despair to innocent Russians across that continental empire. These must all end.

International civil society has almost universally condemned Russia's invasion of Ukraine. With our demands for an immediate and unconditional ceasefire, a negotiated settlement to the war, and the withdrawal of all foreign military troops, we have helped to frame and apply international pressure to end this unjustified and tragic war. No one should be sacrificed or displaced while political leaders and diplomats debate the fine points of the negotiated settlement of the war. Negotiations can take place amidst a ceasefire. This must be our immediate demand.

Looking to the future, after the

guns are silenced we will face the shattered remains of the post-Cold War order, especially the continuing existential nuclear and climate existential threats. Recalling that NATO's expansion to Russia's borders was a contributing cause of the Ukrainian disaster and the long record of devastating U.S. imperial wars, Americans would do well to approach the new era with humility.

Putin has given us new lessons about the catastrophic perils of the arrogance of power. Slow though the restoration of trust and normal diplomatic relations will be, we will face the urgent necessity of Common Security negotiations. The imperatives will be to replace the new ice age of a Cold War with a new Euro-Atlantic order in which no nation seeks to ensure its security at the expense of other nations. This was the promise of initial post-Cold War diplomacy, including the 1997 NATO-Russia Founding Act. And humanity will be sleepwalking to its doom unless the great powers negotiate nuclear disarmament, and to collaborate to stanch the climate chaos that haunts humanity's future.

From END Info 31

Lakenheath added to nuclear weapon storage site upgrades

Hans Kristensen

US Defense Department documents show that NATO has quietly added the United Kingdom to the list of nuclear weapons storage locations that are being upgraded.

The documents do not identify the specific facility, but it is believed to be the US Air Base at RAF Lakenheath in southeast England approximately 100 kilometers northeast of London.

Previous budget documents listed "special weapons" storage sites in Belgium, Germany, Italy, the Netherlands, and Turkey as receiving upgrades under a 13-year NATO investment program. The Biden administration's FY2023 defense budget request adds "the UK" to the list (see image below).

RAF Lakenheath was not on the list of "active sites" in the 2016 contract for the upgrade of the nuclear weapons storage site in Europe. The budget documents indicate the base has since been added to the list.

The US Air Force used to store nuclear gravity bombs at Lakenheath, which in the 1990s was equipped with 33 underground storage vaults. By the early 2000s, there were a total of 110 B61 gravity bombs in the vaults for delivery by F-15E aircraft of the 48th Fighter Wing.

In 2008, I disclosed that the

nuclear weapons had been withdrawn from RAF Lakenheath, the first time since 1954 that the United States did not store nuclear weapons in the United Kingdom.

What's Going On?

The addition of the United Kingdom to the list of nuclear storage locations being upgraded in Europe signals a change in the nuclear status of RAF Lakenheath. It is unclear if nuclear weapons have been returned to the base yet or NATO is upgrading the base to be capable of receiving nuclear weapons in the future if necessary.

After nuclear weapons were withdrawn nearly two decades ago, the empty storage vaults were kept in caretaker status. The F-15Es fighter-bombers retained their nuclear capability but at a lower operational level. In recent years there have been rumors about nuclear exercises at the base.

The nuclear upgrade comes as RAF Lakenheath is preparing to become the first US Air Force base in Europe equipped with the nuclear-capable F-35A Lightning. The first of the fifth-generation fighter-bombers arrived in December 2021. A total of 24 F-35As will form the 495th Fighter Squadron of the 48th Fighter Wing at the base.

The US Air Force is scheduled to begin training the nuclear units in Europe within the next year to receive the new B61-12 guided nuclear bomb that will begin full-scale production next month. It is possible the first B61-12 bombs will be shipped to Europe in 2023, where they will replace the B61-3/-4 bombs currently deployed there.

Given NATO's cautious nuclear response to Russia's nuclear saber rattling at the start of its invasion of Ukraine, it would be odd if the nuclear upgrade at RAF Lakenheath reflected plans to deploy additional US nuclear bombs to Europe. FAS estimates there currently are roughly 100 nuclear bombs deployed at six air bases in five European countries.

NATO Secretary General Jens Stoltenberg declared in December 2021, that "we have no plans of stationing any nuclear weapons in any other countries than we already have these nuclear weapons as part of our deterrence and that… have been there for many, many years." Unless NATO has changed its plans since, that seems to be a clear signal that there are currently no plans to deploy nuclear weapons to RAF Lakenheath for now (see map below).

Rather, the upgrade at RAF Lakenheath could potentially be intended to increase the flexibility of the existing nuclear deployment within Europe, without increasing the number of weapons. Adding RAF Lakenheath as an active site would potentially allow it to receive nuclear weapons from other existing locations in Europe, if that became necessary. Such a contingency could potentially involve receiving weapons withdrawn from Turkey. There are unconfirmed rumors that many of the weapons at Incirlik Air Base in Turkey have already been withdrawn and moved to other bases in Europe.

Readying RAF Lakenheath could potentially also be intended to better realign the overall nuclear posture in Europe with the rapidly deteriorating relations with Russia. This is a delicate issue because changes in NATO's nuclear posture in Europe might trigger retaliatory changes in Russia's nuclear posture, including potentially deployment of nuclear weapons to Belarus, which recently changed its constitution to allow for just that.

First published at:
https://fas.org/blogs/security/2022/04/lakenheath-air-base-added-to-nuclear-weapons-storage-site-upgrades/

Reproduced with permission of the author.

Subscribe to END Info

To be added to the email distribution list or to discuss how to receive printed copies of the newsletter, contact: **tomunterrainer@russfound.org**
To read previous issues of END Info visit: **www.spokesmanbooks.org**
Visit **www.endinfo.net** for web-based versions of recent articles.

Bloomsbury Chapter of the Bertrand Russell Society

Portrait by Hans Erni, 1960

The Bloomsbury Chapter welcomes all those who are curious about and interested in the philosopher and activist, Bertrand Russell. It is an online and, occasionally, in person community exploring his life, work and ideas, with the intention of making them widely accessible. If you have an idea or suggestion, please get in touch. The Bloomsbury Chapter, rooted in Britain, is connected to the worldwide Bertrand Russell Society. Russell lived in Bloomsbury for some years and he has many associations with this part of London. It is fitting that the Bloomsbury Chapter was launched at Conway Hall, Red Lion Square, in May 2022 to mark the 150th anniversary of Russell's birth.

Contact: tonysimpson@russfound.org | Twitter: @BloomsburyChap

Making Palestine's History

by Jehan Helou

Jehan Helou's book 'tells stories of women freedom fighters in their own words, stories untold except maybe to their families and in female circles, even though they are stories that helped determine the course of the Palestinian cause. Much more than novels or tales, these stories are closer to the experiences which must be used in new studies and analyses of the Palestinian Revolution and its stages, and for Palestinian history in general.'

Juheina Khaldieh,
As Safir newspaper, Lebanon

£14.99 | 242 Pages | ISBN: 978 0 85124 9056

Jehan Helou was born in Haifa in 1943. Soon, al Nakba uprooted her family to Lebanon. For long years she was a pioneer in the Palestinian national struggle and the women's liberation movement. More recently, her fervour is directed towards children's culture; she is president of the Palestinian section of the International Board on Books for Young People.

www.spokesmanbooks.org